*A Practical Guide to
Crafting Spell Jars for
Abundance, Luck,
Protection, and More*

Spell
Jars
for the
Modern
Witch

Minerva Siegel

Published by:
ULYSSES PRESS
PO Box 3440
Berkeley, CA 94703
www.ulyssespress.com

ISBN: 978-1-64604-495-5
Library of Congress Control Number: 2023930759

Printed in China
10 9 8 7 6 5 4 3 2 1

Acquisitions editor: Kierra Sondereker
Managing editor: Claire Chun
Editor: Renee Rutledge
Proofreader: Barbara Schultz
Front cover design: Amy King
Interior design and layout: what!design @ whatweb.com
Production: Yesenia Garcia-Lopez
Artwork: shutterstock.com

NOTE TO READERS: This book has been written and published strictly for informational and educational purposes only. It is not intended to serve as medical advice or to be any form of medical treatment. You should always consult your physician before altering or changing any aspect of your medical treatment and/or undertaking a diet regimen, including the guidelines as described in this book. Do not stop or change any prescription medications without the guidance and advice of your physician. Any use of the information in this book is made on the reader's good judgment after consulting with his or her physician and is the reader's sole responsibility. This book is not intended to diagnose or treat any medical condition and is not a substitute for a physician.

This book is independently authored and published and no sponsorship or endorsement of this book by, and no affiliation with, any trademarked brands or other products mentioned within is claimed or suggested. All trademarks that appear in ingredient lists and elsewhere in this book belong to their respective owners and are used here for informational purposes only. The author and publisher encourage readers to patronize the brands mentioned in this book.

For Max, who—in true Taurus sun, Virgo stellium fashion—doesn't believe in magick, but is brimming with it nonetheless. Thank you for being my biggest ally and cheerleader, both in sickness and in health.

Affectionately yours,

Toad-wife

Contents

Introduction

Spell jars, quite simply, are spells crafted and contained inside bottles or jars, though their power extends far beyond those physical confines. Sometimes referred to as "witch bottles," spell jars serve as tangible visual reminders of the spells' intent (that is, of your goals, dreams, and ambitions) to keep you focused and motivated. Spellcrafting in jars is a historic practice dating back at least to the Elizabethan era, though evidence of suspected witch bottles dates back much further. In general, spell jars are best used for spells that will have long-term, lasting effects. Because they're so neatly contained, the magick within is easy to refresh and recharge periodically to maintain its power.

The History of Witch Bottles

Jar spellcrafting is a magickal practice dating back to at least the sixteenth century, though jars and vials from as early as the medieval period, containing small bird and mammal bones along with other trinkets and oddities have been found throughout England and Scandinavia. Pre-seventeenth-century bottles are speculated to have been charm bottles used to ward off mythical creatures and evil, but concrete evidence of witch bottles and their intentions appears in the seventeenth century, so this is when the practice of creating witch bottles is officially considered to have begun.

It's just a matter of evidence; we don't know for certain what the purpose of the Saxon and Scandinavian bottles filled with oddities were used for, but their parallels to later witch bottles are very notable.

Many examples of witch bottles from the Elizabethan era have been excavated in England. One of the earliest literary mentions of spell jars occurred in 1681, in a book by Joseph Glanvill titled *Full and Plain Evidence Concerning Witches and Apparitions*. This book added fuel to the anti-witchcraft furor of the time and heavily influenced the judiciary proceedings of the notorious Salem Witch Trials of 1692 to 1693 in colonial Massachusetts, which found thirty people guilty of witchcraft. Nineteen of them were hung, and one man, Giles Corey, was pressed to death by a weighted board during interrogation. At least five other people died while incarcerated.

Colonial Witch Bottles

A spell jar known as the Essington witch bottle was found in the early 1970s on a Civil War site in Delaware County, Pennsylvania, by archaeologist Marshall Joseph Becker. It was found buried in a hole beside the foundation of a residence that was originally built for Johan Printz, who headed Pennsylvania's first colonial government. The witch bottle is known to have been created around 1740, when Quakers with the last name of Taylor were tenants of the residence. The spell jar is thought to have been crafted to counteract evil forms of witchcraft and curses. Since finding the Essington witch bottle, Becker has identified other eighteenth-and nineteenth-century spell jars throughout the United States.

Bellarmines

Some of the earliest known examples of witch bottles are thought to have been created by frightened, angry Protestants and practitioners of folk magick to punish and repel a particularly ruthless Italian Catholic inquisitor named Robert Bellarmine. A notorious enemy of free thought, Bellarmine not only personally tried, in the name of the Catholic Church, to dissuade the legendary and brilliant astronomer, engineer, and physicist Galileo from his work, he also served as a judge in the trial of philosopher and cosmologist Giordano Bruno. During the trial set forth by the Roman Catholic Inquisition, Bruno was found guilty of heresy and subsequently burned alive at the stake. Many now regard him as a martyr for science and free thought.

Seventeenth-century spell bottles made from salted stoneware have been found with Robert Bellarmine's bearded likeness embossed on the outside. Often filled with vinegar or sharp objects such as pins, needles, and thorns, their crafters took great care to hide these bottles, as it was thought that the spells were only effective as long as they stayed hidden. It was thought that evil would be drawn to and trapped inside the spell jar, where it would then drown in the vinegar or become impaled and die on the sharp objects within. Witch bottles created against Robert Bellarmine, known as "Bellarmines," are still being found under old hearths and during renovations or excavations of seventeenth-century properties.

Of note, Bellarmine was canonized as a saint by the Catholic Church and is still venerated and celebrated by the Church to this day. Though historical spell jars are primarily known to have been created for protection, to break curses, or to curse others, modern spell jars have an enormous variety of themes and intents. They can be crafted to attract positive things like good luck, love, and prosperity; they can repel negativity and provide spellcrafters with magickal protection from negative energy and spirits; and they can help to create balance and stability to help manifest the best life possible. While the applications of witch bottles have broadened over the centuries, some of their basic features have remained true to tradition.

Beginning Your Spell Jar Crafting Journey

This book will guide you through the entire process of jar spellcrafting and impart magickal knowledge that will help you create powerful, successful spell jars. You'll learn about magickal colors, numbers, and other essential properties. You'll discover how to best align the creation of your spell jars with the moon phases, days of the week, and times of day to amplify their intent and potency. An index of herbs, flowers, and other natural ingredients will help you decide what to include in your spell jars, based on your spells' goals. You'll also learn about the uses and applications of different crystal shapes and varieties so you can confidently use crystals to enhance your spell jars.

I'll also provide you with fifty spell jar recipes to help you start manifesting your goals. Whether you're looking to create spell jars to promote a happy, cohesive family life; attract money, love, friendship, or new opportunities; honor an astrological event; capture the power of the full moon; or promote the well-being of children, pets, or other loved ones, this book has you covered!

Free from dogma or the mention of religious notions such as prayers or deities, the spells within this guidebook are consciously gender-neutral and spiritually inclusive. Feel free to alter or add to these spells in ways that resonate with you and your own ethics, practices, and personal beliefs. After all, the only rules to spellcasting are the ones you place upon yourself and your craft.

Part 1

Getting Started
with the
Fundamentals
of Magick

Magickal Basics

Finding Your Own Path

Spellwork is a practice performed by people of many different spiritualities and religions. It's a common misconception that everyone who practices magick identifies as a witch, and that all witches are Wiccan. This simply isn't true. Some spellcasters identify as warlocks, druids, or the like. Wicca is a religion created in the twentieth century. It's eclectically based on a wide variety of pagan and hermetic theology, themes, and principles. I practiced Wicca for a couple of years, when I first started venturing outside of the fanatical sect of evangelicalism I had been brought up in, to explore my attraction to magick and the spirituality of the natural world.

At the time, Wiccan books were all I could easily find, so that's where I began my own personal spiritual journey. After a couple of years spent closely following traditional books on Wicca, I noticed that some parts of it felt out of alignment with my own intuitive inclinations and ideas, so I began researching magickal practices and spiritual thought outside of the Wiccan sphere. I experimented with different witchcraft practices. I stuck with and pursued more deeply that which felt right to me, and moved on from what didn't.

I learned about so many different aspects of witchcraft, and with that exploration came knowledge about cultural appropriation. Some practices are considered "closed," meaning that the majority of people from the cultures from which these practices originate don't want others outside of that cultural background to partake in them. I encourage you to educate yourself on cultural appropriation in witchcraft and modern spirituality. I don't want to speak for people of color, because as a white woman, I'm obviously not entitled to do so. So rather than go into specific examples and explanations of cultural appropriation in witchcraft, please do your research. Listen to and heed the majority opinion coming from the cultures from which the closed practices originate.

I also encourage you to explore your own cultural background and any spiritual practices that may be customary to your lineage. Personally, I'm half Lithuanian, a quarter French, and a quarter British. Lately, I've been researching Lithuanian folk magick and spirituality, and familiarizing myself with the traditions and lore that my Lithuanian great-grandmother shared with me as a young child. Learn about your roots and go on your own journey of self-discovery! Take what resonates, and leave what doesn't.

That's one of the absolute beauties of witchcraft: the only rules to witchcraft are the ones you place upon yourself. Personally, I don't worship deities or subscribe to any religion. That's not to say that I think those who do so are "incorrect" or "lost." We all have our own paths and intuitive attractions and connections, and it's perfectly okay if the way I manifest a divine connection in my own life is different from yours. Our beliefs don't have to be the same, or even similar, to be valid. What matters is the end result—that we fall into alignment with our highest vibe. This is when we're most powerful and in tune, and can manifest the most magick in our lives.

There are countless forms of witchcraft; explaining and exploring the many types of pagan, cultural, religious, secular, eclectic, and other kinds of witchcraft could fill numerous tomes. I took classes on comparative mythology and theologies, and I really recommend continuing your education in other religions and spiritualities, too! You don't have to personally subscribe to different beliefs to learn about, appreciate, and understand them.

This edification can benefit your own spiritual practice and help you discover more about your own personal truths. At the very least, continuing your education on other religions, worldwide spiritualities, and spiritual customs will help you understand others, appreciate diversity, and give you a more helpful global perspective.

Enhancing Your Psychic Sensitivities

We all know of the five physical senses: sight, hearing, touch, taste, and smell. In addition to those five senses, each of us has six "extra" senses that we experience intuitively, or on a spiritual level: clairvoyance, clairaudience, clairsentience, clairalience, clairgustance, and claircognizance. People usually don't experience these senses evenly. Some may be more dominant for you than others. We all have natural aptitudes; some senses come to us more naturally than others. But never fear! You can work to develop each of these senses so that you can connect with spiritual realms and beings more clearly. Let's explore these intuitive senses and learn how you can personally enhance yours.

Clairvoyance: Intuitive Seeing

Clairvoyance often involves seeing visions, such as scenes or small glimpses of the past, present, or future. You're probably familiar with this sense because it's so often depicted in movies and other media. While perhaps some people experience clairvoyance in a dramatic way à la *That's So Raven*, visions can be as simple as a significant, meaningful image popping into your intuitive mind. People who are visual learners or in careers that are predominantly focused on visuals, such as artists and interior decorators, are likely to have clairvoyance as their main intuitive sense.

Clairaudience: Intuitive Hearing

Clairaudience refers to intuitively hearing music, words, or voices that aren't coming from the physical realm. Hearing children's laughter coming from the spiritual realm is often reported in haunted, old homes, but people with clairaudience as their dominant sense can be attuned to hearing all kinds of unearthly sounds and noises.

You might be familiar with electronic voice phenomenon, or EVP. To catch evidence of EVP, ghost hunters and parapsychologists go into haunted spaces and collect audio recordings on machines. When played, these recordings sometimes reveal sounds and voices that weren't discernible to the human ear at the time they were collected. It's thought that spirits exist on different vibrational planes, so it takes an enormous amount of effort and energy for them to communicate in a vocal way on frequencies that humans can hear. It's said that technology has an easier time picking up on the frequencies on which spirits communicate, so collecting EVPs can help bridge the communication gap between the spirit world and our physical realm.

The best method to heighten your clairaudience is simply to listen. I don't mean "listen" in an everyday, commonplace way, but really put magickal intent into the practice of listening. Make yourself comfortable in a spiritual space, whether that's at an altar (for more on creating a ritual space, see page 31), outside in nature, in a peaceful, secluded spot, or in a dwelling or structure that's known to have spiritual activity or hauntings.

If you're going to a known haunted area, make sure you're spiritually protected. While many spirits and spiritual entities aren't malicious, the fact is that if spirits are strong enough to manifest in this realm to the point that the area they haunt is known for their activity, there's the potential that they could be strong enough to be dangerous or cause trouble. While these areas are often the best places to pick up EVP evidence and clairaudience messages, remember to be safe! The spell jar recipes called Banish Bad Vibes on page 135 and Protect Your Peace (A Spell Jar for Empaths) on page 141 can help!

Start tuning in to your clairaudience by sitting in your chosen spot, closing your eyes to decrease visual stimuli and putting the focus on your auditory sense, and listening. Notice every little sound, but don't focus on them for too long. Let them come and go from your mind. Stay open to new sounds that come forward. Meditate in this way for a while to build your clairaudience. Eventually, you may just start picking up on spiritual sounds from beyond the physical plane. Listen for music, voices, words, repetitive banging, and other sounds. If you do this regularly, you'll heighten your sense of clairaudience.

Clairsentience: Intuitive Feeling

Have you ever walked by a building and instantly gotten bad vibes from it, even though there's nothing to indicate negativity from just visually looking at it? Hunches and gut feelings fall under the clairsentience sensory umbrella. Clairsentience refers to intuitive feelings. It's thought places and even objects tied to strong emotions or intense events hold residual energy

Spell Jars for the Modern Witch

from those feelings and events, which people with well-developed clairsentience can pick up on. This can apply to people, too; clairsentience can include the ability to intuitively sense the aura and energetic vibrations other people emit. If you describe yourself as an empath, or someone who picks up on others' pain, joy, and feelings easily, you probably have great clairsentience. Those with a strong connection to this sense tend to be empathetic, compassionate people drawn to caregiving careers.

To develop this sense, pay attention to any gut feelings you experience. If you get bad or good vibes from a person, place, or object, don't ignore them. These types of feelings are often easy to explain away and ignore, but when you pay attention to them and give them more credence, your clairsentience becomes a more dominant sense for you. Over time, you'll start trusting your clairsentience more, which will make you even more in tune with it.

Clairalience: Intuitive Smelling

It's well known that scent is strongly tied to memory. For example, people often report intuitively smelling scents like the perfume or cologne of a loved one who's passed on. Even though there's no physical source of the smell, they get a strong waft of it, which triggers the memory of their loved one. These people also report feeling a sense of comfort from this experience. They feel as though their loved one is communicating that they're still with them in some form. People who sense these intuitive smells have a strong sense of clairalience. It's thought that spirits manifest scents like this so that people connect with them, making it possible to send messages or make people aware of their presence.

I have experience with this sense. When my husband and I bought our dream home—a four-story Edwardian house built in 1904—it came with residual energy from people who lived there before us. Before I spiritually purified the home to clear that residual energy and placed protective wards (objects charmed to become psychokinetic shields that deflect negative energy) strategically around the property, I used to get a strong waft of some sort of old-fashioned aftershave in the mornings while getting ready for the day. I never caught the scent during any other time of day, only in the mornings before 9 a.m. In my mind's eye, I'd get a quick vision of the side view of a man bent over a sink, shaving. I did some digging and found a few old photos of the bathroom from the sixties, before it was remodeled; the sink looked exactly the same as it did in my vision. I was picking up on the imprinted energy of a former inhabitant's morning routine, and scent was a major component to these visions. This is an example of clairalience!

The best way to develop this sense is to pay closer attention to the scents you experience, and how they make you feel. Stop to smell the roses! What does their scent remind you of? What comes to mind when you smell them? How does the scent make you feel?

Spell Jars for the Modern Witch

Analyze a wide variety of smells. Is your neighbor cutting the grass? Does that remind you of your childhood, when your dad would ask you to mow the lawn before he gave you an allowance? Maybe you're baking a pie. Perhaps that conjures memories of your grandmother teaching you to bake as you stood on tippy toes to get involved. Think of the words that come to mind when you smell freshly baked pie: Home? Comfort? Family? Togetherness? Paying more attention to the scents around you and what you personally associate them with will help build your sense of clairalience. You'll soon start becoming more aware and discerning of intuitive scents with otherworldly sources.

Clairgustance: Intuitive Tasting

This sense may be a little more uncommon than the others, but it does show up in people who have strong emotional ties or memories linked to taste. Clairgustance is similar to clairalience in that spirits of people you knew in life who have passed on may manifest a taste as a way to contact you. Perhaps your late grandfather had a favorite mixed drink he enjoyed every time you went out to a restaurant. If you suddenly experience the taste of that mixed drink, without anything in the physical world stimulating that sense, you may be experiencing clairgustance.

My advice for developing this sense is similar to my advice for developing clairalience: pay closer attention to your sense of taste. Analyze flavors carefully in terms of what they represent to you and what they bring to mind. Take a sip of tart lemonade. What does it make you think of? Summertime and sunshine?

How does that taste make you feel? Energized? Happy? Carefree? Experience and analyze a wide variety of flavors and mouthfeels to develop your clairgustance. When you notice the emotional and mental associations that connect with different tastes, you'll become more open to receiving spiritual messages and signs via clairgustance.

Claircognizance: Intuitive Knowing

Have you ever known something for certain in a way you can't explain? You have no way of actually knowing it, but everything in you is saying it's a fact. Spiritual and religious leaders often claim to know things, despite there being no practical way for them to truly know. These occurrences could, perhaps, be examples of claircognizance.

You may have heard of people who have warned others to take a different route home or skip an event. They had no practical way of knowing that something bad would happen if these people continued on their current trajectory, but they somehow received a strong sense of certainty of such if the people they warned didn't alter their current course. Then, it was later revealed that those people would have been in danger had they gone to the event or not changed their route. Those who'd given the warnings are examples of people with a strong sense of claircognizance.

Many people brush off their sense of claircognizance. They get strong feelings—urges to change trajectory or knowing intuitive truths they can't explain—but rationalize them away because they don't make sense in the physical realm.

To develop your sense of claircognizance, you need to stop brushing off and talking yourself out of intuitive truths. Exercising critical thought in our everyday lives is important, but it's just as important to not rationalize ourselves out of episodes of claircognizance. If you get a strong, sudden urge to take a different path, avoid or connect with a certain person, avoid a situation, or go somewhere, try taking those urges seriously and acting on them. When you see that things turn out well, over time, you'll begin trusting your claircognizance more, strengthening that sense.

Working to consciously develop your psychic senses will help you to strengthen your connections with your own personal magick, which will make you a more powerful and successful spellcaster. Heightening your psychic perception will also attune you to the auras, energies, and vibrations of the people and places around you, and make you more comfortable trusting your intuitive feelings. Developing these senses will help you manifest the most magickal, powerful, confident version of yourself.

Magickal Basics

The Six Steps to Creating a Spell Jar

There are six primary steps to creating a successful spell jar: set your intent, gather the ingredients and tools you'll need for your spell jar, prepare your spellcrafting space, assemble the spell jar, activate the spell, and seal it. Let's take a closer look at each step individually.

Step One: Set Your Intent

In order for your spell jar to be effective, you have to begin with a very clear goal. Are you looking to create a spell jar to stop nightmares? Attract new friendships into your life? Boost your creativity and focus so you can nail a major presentation at work? This isn't the time for generalizations or ambiguity.

For example, saying you want to build a spell jar to attract love isn't quite specific enough. The crystals, flora, and other ingredients and tools you should use change based on what type of love you're looking to invite into your life. Do you want to find long-lasting, romantic love? Are you hoping to strengthen familial bonds and connections? Attract new best friends and platonic soul-connections? Visualize a very clear image of what this spell jar's success looks like to guide and inform the whole creation process.

Step Two: Gather Ingredients and Tools

Once your intent is set and you've chosen the exact goal you want to accomplish with your spell jar, it's time to select a jar and begin deciding which ingredients, tools, and other implements you may want to include in your spellcrafting session.

I encourage you to put a good amount of thought into this, and be thorough. Make sure you have everything you need when beginning your spell to avoid breaking your concentration to fetch something in the middle of it. This would be disruptive and could affect the spell's viability.

I have a natal Capricorn moon and stellium, so naturally I love lists. If you're going off-recipe, feel free to make a list of exactly what ingredients you need, and check off items as you gather them to make sure you're properly prepared.

Selecting the Perfect Jar

I'd be willing to bet that you already have a collection of containers and jars at home that would make excellent spell jars. Mason jars are probably the most commonly used jars for spellcrafting; they're a convenient size (though spell jars can be as large or small as you'd like), they seal well, and they're glass, so they won't degrade or leach chemicals over time like plastic or melt if you decide to use hot wax to seal them. One thing to keep in mind while choosing the perfect jar is that bottles with cork stoppers are best used with dry ingredients only, as liquids such as Moon Water and oils (common spell jar ingredients) can degrade the cork.

Alternative bottles to the standard mason jar include cleaned glass drink bottles or repurposed glass pots that once contained skincare or cosmetic creams. Even ceramic or porcelain containers can be a great option if you seal them well.

Lidded containers carved from crystal are a luxurious option for spell jar creation. I have containers carved from clear quartz that I've used to create long-term spell jars. Clear quartz is a great energy amplifier, so by containing the entire spell in a clear quartz container, its effects and magick are strengthened and amplified. Carved crystal or ceramic containers can be a particularly good option to be covert with your spellcasting if you live in a shared space. These containers look innocuous sitting on a shelf and are less obvious and visually intriguing than a mason jar full of herbs, crystals, and other ingredients.

Around the winter holidays, consider heading to your local craft store to stock up on empty, fillable ornaments. They come in all sorts of festive, fun shapes and are perfect for creating hanging spell jars. Fill them with magickal ingredients and hang them from cabinet pulls, doorknobs, or decorative hooks. They also make great gift-toppers; simply tie them to the handles of gift bags or affix them to gift boxes with string.

Selecting Ingredients and Tools

There are so many different items you can incorporate into a spell jar. Choose what to include thoughtfully, based on the intent of your spell. I like to include crystals in each spell jar to help amplify their energy and potency, or cultivate the sort of energy the spell needs to thrive. See the Crystal Index on page 71 for inspiration!

Most spellcasters feel that it's important to use natural elements consciously in spellwork. Using natural materials consciously can help you attune to the powerful, energies of our world and connect with the might of the magickal elements. Incorporate elements of nature into spell jars by using eggshells, dirt from specific places relevant to the spell, water from natural sources such as streams or collected rainwater, or any number of different dried flora. For a thorough index of natural ingredients and their uses, see page 74.

Including mementos and charms in jar spellwork can give it a more personalized, focused touch. Things like ticket stubs, old wrist bands with memories tied to them, carefully selected tarot cards (see page 53 to learn about tarot card meanings and associations), sentimental or meaningful jewelry, photographs, symbolic charms, written words such as affirmations and intentions, and other little trinkets can be used in your spell jar. I think it always helps to have a biological element (collected and used with permission!) or photograph when doing spells focused on one particular person.

For example, I'm dog-mom to a very sweet, stocky pit bull who was used in illegal dog fighting in her previous life, before I adopted her. She's a very loving, happy dog now, but she's a sensitive soul who has a lot of severe, old injuries that healed poorly because she wasn't given medical care when she needed it. In addition to taking her to specialists and giving her the therapeutic emotional support and reassurance that helps her thrive, I created a spell jar dedicated to promoting her healing and overall wellness.

I brushed her and saved some of the shed hair to include in the jar to direct the magick specifically to her. I also included a little photograph of her I'd taken during a very happy moment to help imbue the spell with the same happy, carefree energy. I added the crystals nephrite jade, bloodstone, black kyanite, jet, and sunstone to promote emotional and energetic healing, letting go of the past, the transmutation of negative energy into positive vibes, and happiness. Cedarwood, marigold, and carnation petals were sprinkled into the jar for protection, healing, and karmic justice. I added a large clear quartz sphere to amplify the energy of the spell, then sealed the jar with wax and a kiss (for love!). I keep this spell jar near her bed.

Selecting Paper and Writing Tools

Whether written or spoken, words have power. I like to incorporate them in most of my spellwork, and that includes the crafting of spell jars. I try to put care into selecting everything from the colors and types of paper to the writing tools I use, choosing ones that best fit the intent of the spell I'm working on. For a Magickal Color Correspondence reference table to help you choose which colors of both paper and ink to use in your spell, see page 49.

I usually prefer to use natural, craft, or recycled papers, but in a pinch, even a sticky note will do! Any writing implement can be used in spellwork: markers, colored pencils, gel pens, etc. You could go outside the box and carve your words into something more substantial to place in the spell jar, such as a small piece of wood or tile. Try out different methods and do whatever feels right to you. Some people use a fountain pen, feather quill, or paintbrush, and make their own ink from flower petals. Here's a basic flower petal ink recipe for you to use as inspiration.

DIY Flower Petal Writing Ink Recipe

* Colorful, fresh nontoxic flower petals, such as cornflower or peony
* Mortar and pestle
* 1 ounce or so of boiling water
* Small stain-resistant jar or bowl to hold the ink
* Thin paintbrush

1. Grind the fresh flower petals with a mortar and pestle to make a paste.

2. Add a small amount of boiling water to the paste and stir until a thin consistency perfect for writing is achieved.

3. Transfer the mixture to a small bowl, and write with it using a thin paintbrush.

Tip: If you accidentally add too much water and your ink becomes too thin, you can leave it to evaporate in the sun for a while.

Other Potential Spellwork Tools

Other tools commonly used in jar spellcrafting include athames, candles, and wands. Athames are ritual daggers often used in spellwork for carving. They can be made with traditional metal or beautiful crystal blades. I find that the crystal blades have a duller point that isn't as effective for carving, but I use them to draw sigils over surfaces without marking or damaging them. For more on creating and using sigils, see page 42. In spell jars, you can use athames to carve sigils or words into any candles or wax used during your spell. I often seal my spell jars with wax and carve small protective or magick-enhancing sigils into the wax.

As I mentioned above, candles and candle wax are often used in jar spellcrafting. The act of lighting a candle before assembling a spell jar brings focus and energy to the process. Personally, I use candles in almost all my spellwork. Lighting and snuffing candles marks the beginning and end of the spellwork session and invites and honors the element of Fire. Fire represents action, change, focus, and passion—all helpful energy to create effective spellwork.

Some people use wands to help focus their magick and energy. Before you balk at the notion of people emphatically waving wands around and expecting physics-defying supernatural acts of levitation or disappearance to occur á la Harry Potter or a magic show, let me quell your skepticism by saying that's not what I'm referring to at all! That kind of wand use is for live action role-playing and games.

Serious spellcrafters use wands to channel and focus their magickal energy or the manifested energy of a spell. Almost anything can be a conduit for such magickal purposes. Some fashion wands from wood or simply use sticks they find outside. Some wands are carved from stone or crystal. Others use polymer clay wands decorated with crystals or intricate carvings. In jar spellcrafting, wands can be used to activate the spell.

Step Three: Prepare the Spellcrafting Space

Most spellcrafters agree that it's important to energetically and spiritually cleanse the immediate space where you'll be performing spellwork. This ensures that no unwanted energies will interfere with or muddle your spell. Essentially, energy cleansing is basic spiritual hygiene. There are several different methods that can be used to accomplish this, and I encourage you to experiment with them! Try out different methods, or combinations of methods, to figure out which ones feel best to you. You don't have to stick to any one method, either. Feel free to change it up depending on your mood or the intent of the spell jar. Let's explore four different methods you can use to spiritually prepare your ritual space.

Sound Cleansing

Sound cleansing is the act of using sound to purify a space. The main thought behind it is that certain frequencies carry through the air and disrupt stagnant, unwanted energy. It's a time-honored cleansing method used by many different cultures around the world, from Gregorian monks who chant at specific frequencies to cultivate a relationship with the divine to the sacred use of Tibetan singing bowls.

Many people believe that specific frequencies are best used for sound cleansing. The easiest way to begin exploring them is to look up videos and playlists online that are created for frequency-specific sound cleansing. I think looking into the nine solfeggio frequencies is a great place to start. Solfeggio frequencies are a series of specific tones that are said to target and heal different parts of the body and aspects of the spirit. The sound-cleansing methods I prefer to use include playing chimes or crystal singing bowls, or simply hand-ringing a small bell. I find sound cleansing to be a very invigorating, stimulating practice that really wakes me up and gets me in the proper headspace for spellcrafting.

Smoke Cleansing

Smoke cleansing is the act of using the smoke from burning herbs or flowers to purify a space. Herbs commonly dried and used to cleanse include cedar, rosemary, mugwort, and white sage.

Today, many people mistakenly refer to the act of burning sage as "smudging," but smudging is a sacred indigenous, closed practice that involves more than simply burning herbs. Being that I'm not of indigenous descent and did not grow up with this practice in my culture, I don't use the term. White sage is commonly used in smoke cleansing, but it's also an herb traditionally used by indigenous people in the culturally sacred act of smudging. Many members of indigenous communities have asked that non indigenous people stop burning sage.

It's a complex issue involving over harvesting and historic and ongoing mistreatment of indigenous communities. It was illegal in the US for indigenous peoples to practice their own religions and cultural traditions, which included the act of burning sage, until the passage of the American Indian Religious Freedom Act in 1978. With all this being said, I'm not a spokesperson for indigenous communities, so I invite you to do your own research into this complex issue and listen to what indigenous people have to say on the subject when deciding which herbs to use in your smoke-cleansing practice. If you do choose to use sage, consider growing it yourself, making sure your source grows sage sustainably, or purchasing it from an indigenous source to support their community.

Smoke cleansing is an ancient practice used around the world by many different cultures. I encourage you to look into your own lineage because it's entirely possible that your ancestors had smoke-cleansing practices of their own! Finding out which dried herbs and flowers they used and how they used them could be a very rewarding process that connects you to your roots and exposes you to a new way of smoke cleansing.

When I cleanse with smoke, I light a dried herb bundle and let it burn until the herbs are smoldering softly. Holding the herbs in a fire-safe container, I walk around the space, making sure the smoke reaches into every nook and cranny. If you'd like to cleanse a small object, you can pass it through the smoke of burning herbs.

Space Cleansing with Visualization

You don't need a lot of stuff to practice spellwork. While some people love collecting large amounts of tools, aids, crystals, singing bowls, and other implements to enhance their spellcrafting, none of it is really necessary to perform spells. Minimalistic spellwork is perfectly okay, too! Acts as simple as saying words with intent, or visualization can be spellwork.

If you don't have other cleansing tools on hand, or you're just looking for a quick, no-frills purification method, consider visualization. You can either close your eyes or focus on a flame. Imagine a bright, powerful, holy light radiating from you and filling the space, chasing negativity and stagnant energy away as it envelops the room.

Space Cleansing with Crystals

My vast collection of crystals is, by far, my most treasured self-care investment. I've been collecting them for over a decade, and even still, their power and usefulness amazes me. My house is full of strategically placed crystals and intricate crystal grids, set up to protect my home from negative energies and entities, cultivate peaceful and easy communication, and help me manifest a focused, creative headspace perfect for productivity.

Each type of crystal or stone has a unique energy and spiritual meaning, and many people, including myself, believe that the shape of the crystal can help direct or amplify its energy in specific ways. For more on crystal shapes and their uses, see the table on page 70.

Selenite is really the master cleansing crystal. A common, inexpensive, and easily accessible crystal, selenite cleanses anything it comes into contact with. I keep selenite spheres or pyramids in every room of my house to keep the energy in them refreshed and unencumbered by negative or iffy vibes. I also keep a selenite stick on top of all my tarot decks to prevent unwanted energy from attaching itself to the cards, so they're always clean and ready to be used.

To cleanse a space with crystals in preparation for a spell jar crafting session, you can simply place selenite in the middle of your crafting space. I prefer to use spheres or pyramids, but any shape will do in a pinch. Alternatively, you can walk around your space with the selenite and recite a cleansing affirmation, such as:

"This space is spiritually purified, an energetic clean slate."

For a boost, you can also incorporate protective crystals, or ones known for transmuting negative or stagnant energy into positive energy, such as jet, black obsidian, black tourmaline, or black kyanite. My personal favorites to use are jet and black kyanite. Their energy feels light and refreshing, whereas tourmalines, hematite, and other types of protective stones and crystals sometimes have a heavier energy that feels a bit too intense for some very sensitive crystal enthusiasts. I encourage you to experiment with different types; sit quietly while holding them in your palm to decide which crystals and stones feel as if they will work best with your own signature energy and aura.

Step Four: Assemble the Spell Jar

It's time to build your spell jar. I often start by adding the written intentions to spell jars (if applicable), because that helps to set a solid tone for the rest of the spell jar's creation. After that, the ingredients are usually added from heaviest or bulkiest to lightest, but that's not an absolute must-do. If I'm creating a spell jar that uses dirt, I usually add the dirt first to create a base for the other ingredients. When making spell jars that use Moon Water, I usually add that ingredient last to submerge all the contents of the spell jar fully. There are no hard-and-fast rules to the assembly of spell jars, so please feel free to assemble yours in the ways that feel most appropriate to you, and in alignment with your own intuition.

Step Five: Activate the Spell Jar

After your spell jar has been assembled, and is full of magickal ingredients and intent, it's time to give it a concentrated boost of magickal energy to activate it and set its power into action. There are several ways of doing this: through visualization; by using athames, wands, or clear quartz points; by simply shaking the jar; or by adding essential oils to the spell jar. Sunlight and moonlight can also be used to activate spells. Sometimes, activation can be performed after the jar is sealed. For example, if the activation method involves shaking the jar and its contents, it's best to do this after the jar is sealed. However, sometimes spell jars can be activated by adding essential oils to the contents, so you'd have to make sealing your spell jar the final step in that instance.

Using visualization techniques to activate your spell jars is a very accessible method, as it requires no tools at all. To do this, hold the jar so both palms are touching it. Many people believe that your palms are energy centers that transfer and receive magick, which is why it's important to make contact with the spell jar using your palms. Close your eyes to concentrate better, or focus intently on the jar, and envision a bright sphere of powerful energy forming in the center of your body. Take time to concentrate on building that energy, and then, when you feel ready, imagine that manifested power flowing through your palms and energizing your spell.

Another way of activating a spell jar is to use an athame, wand, or clear quartz point. Athames are ritual blades most often used to carve sigils or words during spells, but some people also use them as a sort of wand to direct their energy. They can be made from metals, wood, or carved from crystals.

Wands are elongated, pointed tools for directing magick, and can be made from crystal, clay, wood, metal—the sky's the limit, really. The most important aspect when choosing a wand is that you feel a spiritual connection to it. Though meeting your perfect wand may not instigate the sort of energetic, swirling whirlwind, orchestral symphony, and supernatural spotlight you'd see in a Harry Potter film, you'll know when you have a perfect wand for you because using it will feel very natural and easy.

Clear quartz is the great energy amplifier of the crystal world. It's excellent at directing and enhancing magick, which makes it one of the best crystals to use in activating spells. To activate a spell jar, hold your athame, wand, or clear quartz point, manifest energy in the same way as described in the visualization technique above, and then you can either tap the jar to transfer your magick or hold the tip of your activation tool against the jar for any length of time.

Another very accessible, easy way to activate a spell jar is to simply shake it. Be mindful of your ingredients when deciding whether or not to use this method. You may not want to employ this one if your jar contains something like grandma's heirloom jewelry and a bunch of sharp crystals that could scratch it, or small herbs that could become lodged in the jewelry and make a mess! However, if your jar is well-sealed and its contents can withstand some movement, swirling or shaking the jar to stir up its contents will set your magick into kinetic motion and activate your spell jar.

Essential or blessed oils (blessed oils are oils that are prayed over or otherwise transformed through spiritual means to become holy or sacred) can be added to spell jars as the final ingredient to activate their magick. Choose which essential oil to use based on the goal of your spell; use the information in the section titled Essential Oils Commonly Used in Spellwork Index on page 77 to help guide you.

Step Six: Seal the Spell Jar

There are a few different ways to seal your finished spell jar. Outer and inner wax sealing, sealing with tape, cloth sealing, and using sigils to seal the spell jar spiritually are the most commonly used methods, but copper electroforming is another great option that's best used on spell jars you know you'll want sealed permanently.

Outer Wax Sealing

Wax methods are best for spell jars that will be kept out of the heat and sun because if they're exposed to either, they can make a big mess. So consider where you want to keep your spell jar before committing to this method. Another thing to consider is the color of the wax you want to use. I base the color of the wax on the intent of the spell jar. Use the color table on page 49 to help you decide which color corresponds best with the goal of your spell.

When creating a small spell jar, such as one in a wearable necklace vial, I like to light a candle during the creation of the spell jar, then use wax drippings from that candle to seal the jar. To do this, tip your candle so that the wax pours over the sealed jar's cork or lid. If your jar is large, it may take quite a lot of wax, so consider buying bars of wax to melt.

Personally, I like using wax bars meant for wax-sealing letters and documents because it's easy to control the wax flow and amount. If you don't want the contents of your spell jar to be visible, you can use enough wax during the sealing process to coat the jar as much as desired and obscure its contents from view.

Inner Wax Sealing

The inner wax sealing method is a little trickier to get right. You have to work very quickly before the wax dries, and working quickly can lead to messes. But practice makes perfect! To do this sealing method, carefully drip wax around the inner rim of your jar, then quickly seal it before it dries so that the wax binds the lid or cork to the jar. Sometimes, I accidentally drip wax into the contents of the spell jar when performing the inner seal method. If this happens to you, don't worry about it! Your spell jar is still effective.

Sealing with Tape

Using tape is an easy, accessible way to seal your jar. Washi tape comes in so many different colors and prints but may not have as much longevity as something more heavy-duty, like duct tape. I've found that the efficacy of washi tape in spell jar sealing depends on the type of jar or bottle used and the environment the spell jar is kept in. For example, sealing a jar with washi tape might not be the best method if you plan on burying the jar, anointing it with oils, or keeping it in a moist environment; moisture and oils will degrade the adhesive. If you're looking for a really tough seal and aren't particularly concerned with aesthetics, duct tape is certainly the way to go. I have used duct tape to seal spell jars designed to cut ties with other people. It can be a great way to represent permanence and strength.

Cloth Sealing

This is a simple, cottagecore-approved method for sealing spell jars. It's best for spell jars that don't contain any fresh ingredients that could cause odors as they age because cloth doesn't create as strong of a seal as other methods. Consider using this method for spell jars that you'll want to open up to refresh regularly, or for short-term spell jars.

To seal with cloth, take a bandana or scrap of cloth (depending on the size of the jar) and place it over the jar's opening. Place a rubber band or tie string around the lip of the jar so the cloth stays put. Pull on the edges of the fabric to tighten the seal, if necessary.

Sigils

Sigils are symbols imbued with specific magick by their creator. For example, sigils can be created with the purpose of protection, spell amplification, or to ward off negative or interfering influences. There are many different methods for creating sigils, but the most common one is the reduction method.

To create a sigil using the reduction method, write down the goal of your spell, an affirmation relating to the spell, or a word that you feel encompasses the spell. I like to work with affirmations when creating sigils. Below is a personal example for a spell created to protect me from nightmares.

Start by writing the affirmation:

I am protected while I sleep.

Then, cross out the vowels, which leaves:

m p r t c t d w h l s l p

Reduce this further by removing repeated letters to end up with:

m p r t c d w h l s

Now for the fun part! Artistically and intuitively combine these letters into a single sigil. The image below is an example of a sigil a drew using the affirmation to protect me from nightmares.

m p r t c d w h l s

Look for similar shapes within letters to find opportunities to combine letters, saving space and helping to make the sigil more obscure. Feel free to sketch on scrap paper and try out different ways of combining these letters until you settle on a sigil that intuitively resonates with you. This sigil can then be drawn on paper and added into your spell jar, or used to seal it by drawing or etching the sigil onto the bottle, inside the cap of the bottle, or on top of the bottle cap.

Copper Electroforming

Electroforming is the process of fusing copper onto an object electrically. Very specific equipment and materials are required for this process, and it's by far the costliest method I've used to seal a spell jar, but it can be so beautiful! This method is for spell jars that you want permanently sealed.

One of my best friends is artist Linnae Dufresne. She creates beautiful, witchy, electroplated objects and jewelry. When one of my rescue dogs died, I knew I wanted to create a special memorial jar for her using fur I'd saved, along with her cremains, baby teeth, and other carefully curated ingredients. I considered using the wax sealing method, but I knew I'd keep that very special memorial spell jar for the rest of my life, and I was concerned that wax may eventually melt, or that the jar may need to survive a move someday. I wanted a more permanent method to seal the spell bottle—one that felt respectful. (In other words, I didn't want to use duct tape to seal this very special jar containing all that's tangibly left of my beloved dog.)

I told Linnae about the spell jar I was creating, and she immediately offered to electroform it for me. I mailed the jar to her, and she sealed it, decorated it, and added beautiful, meaningful crystals to it using the electroforming process. I'm so grateful to her for it; it's absolutely perfect. The memorial spell jar sits pride of place on my parlor mantle beside the beetle-cleaned, preserved skull of my beloved late mastiff.

Decoration Options

The sky is really the limit as far as decorating your spell jar goes! You can make it a maximalist marvel or keep it minimalistic and utilitarian. If you do choose to decorate your finished spell jar, keep your spell's intent in mind while doing so. I prefer to decorate them in ways that either amplify or synchronize with the energy and theme of the spell.

A particularly pretty way to decorate spell jars is with wax and dried herbs or flowers. To do this, drip drops of wax onto the bottle and press your flora to it quickly before the wax dries so it affixes securely. Consider using the same type of flora to decorate the jar that was used inside the spell jar for magickal continuity.

Charms or beads can be affixed to the jar using twine, thread, or string. For example, when creating a spell jar to honor the full moon, you could use string to attach a lunar charm or pendant, tying it around the top of the jar with a neat bow. Personally, I like attaching charms to spell bottles because it helps me keep track of the theme and goal of each jar, as I make quite a few of them! The charms act as a label reminding me of the spell's purpose, but they're also ambiguous enough that I can maintain an element of secrecy if someone should happen to see the spell jar. Someone unfamiliar with the nature of the spell won't necessarily guess what it's for just by seeing a charm attached to the outside of the bottle.

Spell bottles, depending on the texture and type of jar used, can also be decorated with dripped wax, meaningful sigils or other symbols, hot glue, glitter, washi tape, etc. Be creative and experiment!

How to Dismantle Spell Jars

Spell jars can last for whatever length of time feels right to you. I have some spell jars, such as memorial jars, that are permanent. Other bottles contain long-term spells that I regularly recharge to maintain their magickal effects, and some spell jars can be disposed of once their desired effects have materialized and you no longer have need for them.

To dismantle one properly, it's most important to consider the spell jar's ingredients to make sure you're disposing of them safely and in an environmentally friendly way. Personally, I burn the written intentions along with the flora used in the jar whenever it's safe to do so. I have a large, fire-safe, cast-iron dutch oven I use just for that purpose. I then take the ashes and mix them with sea salt to create magickal Black Salt, a powerful protector and spell ingredient.

Some spell jars call for dirt to be used; I simply pour out the dirt and bury it, returning it to the earth. Often, I'll bury the crystals used in spell jars, too. My husband often jokes that one day, we're going to find ourselves needing a contractor to do work on our land, and they'll be shocked to unearth all the buried crystals and spell elements there. What an interesting conversation that will be! Hopefully, they're not stumbled upon until long after we're gone, and locals will make up fabled stories about the witch who must have lived here.

Any elements from the spell jar that I want to keep, such as jewelry, photos, or crystals, I cleanse by using sacred smoke, by placing the cleansing crystal selenite on top of them for a length of time, or by leaving them in the light of the moon overnight. The full moon is best for cleansing, but any phase during which the moon is visible will do in a pinch.

When disposing of spell jars that were used for banishment, or to cut ties with someone, I bury the jars, unopened, somewhere far away from my home. It's important that any energy associated with them—even the energy used to banish them—isn't left in your home or personal space indefinitely. If you need to dismantle it and retain some element from a spell jar used for banishment, perform this act away from your home and cleanse the element you want to keep very thoroughly. Again, though, I really recommend just cutting your losses and getting rid of all elements used in such a jar.

Typically, I like to reuse the jars from these spells, but thoughtfully. I make sure I use them for similar spells. For instance, I'll take a bottle from a spell jar that was created to encourage a positive, harmonious collaboration at work, cleanse it thoroughly with smoke or moonlight, and repurpose it as the jar for a spell intended to help cultivate harmony and positive communication at home. The goals of both spells are similar enough that any residual energy left attached to the jar won't muddle or interfere with the new spell.

However, I'd never take a spell jar that was used for banishment and then use it for a completely different spell, like one intended to help me reconnect with a loved one. Reuse bottles for similar spells, but any spell jars that have heavy or cumbersome energy, such as ones used in cutting ties with someone, cleanse very well or consider not reusing in magick.

Helpful Correspondences and Associations

The possibilities for spell jar ingredients are truly endless. Once you've set your intentions, deciding what components to add to your jar to create the spell can sometimes seem daunting! This section of the book contains fundamental magickal knowledge that will take away that cloudy mystery and uncertainty to help you craft your own personal off-recipe spell jars.

The information here can also help you decide how to time the creation of your spell jars based on the intent of your spell. For instance, if you're creating a spell jar to help you regain focus and recommit to a goal you've lost sight of, you could use the information in these tables to determine that the best time to create such a spell jar would be during a New Moon, in December, on a Wednesday, and/or at dawn.

Experiment! Learn! Have fun! Try incorporating different elements to your spell jar creation process, like chakra symbols, tarot cards, or a certain number of items based on the information found in the Number Correspondences table (see page 50). Find the elements that best resonate with your energy, practice, and goals. Spellcrafting is a personal thing; what matters most in determining a spell's success is that the crafter truly feels a connection to it. If you don't put your own authentic magick and heart into the process, you won't see such powerful results. Happy spell jar crafting!

Color Correspondences

Black	Binding spells, divination, protection, transformation
White	Spiritual cleansing and purification; an all-purpose color when used in candle magic
Red	Ambition, courage, passion, strength
Orange	Confidence, ego, ethics, fairness and justice
Yellow	Communication, joy, the intellect
Green	Beauty, good luck, growth, prosperity
Blue	Emotional healing, psychic enhancement, truth
Purple	Power, psychic enhancement
Silver	Intuition enhancement, lunar magick
Gold	Financial success, good luck, longevity, solar magick

Element Correspondences

	Air	Earth	Water	Fire
Glyph	△	▽	▽	△
Direction	East	North	West	South
Lunar Phase	Waxing Moon	New Moon	Waning Moon	Full Moon
Season	Spring	Winter	Autumn	Summer
Time of Day	Sunrise	Midnight	Sunset	Noon
Magickal Tool	Athame	Pentacle	Chalice	Wand
Elemental Spirit	Sylphs	Gnomes	Undines	Mythical Salamanders
Color	Yellow	Green	Blue	Red

Number Correspondences

I	New beginnings, naivety, optimism	VI	Communication, cooperation
II	Balance, choices, partnerships and unions	VII	Recovery, reflection, rest
III	Creativity, expression	VIII	Accomplishment, mastery
IV	Grounded energy, home, stability	IX	Abundance, fulfillment
V	Conflict, sudden changes	X	Completion, cycles, transitions

Spell Jars for the Modern Witch

Crown Chakra

Sanskrit	Sahasrara (in English: "Thousand-Petaled")	**Life Area**	Consciousness
Location	Top of head	**Crystals**	Blue apatite, moonstone
Affirmation	"I understand."	**Flora**	Jasmine, white lily

Third Eye Chakra

Sanskrit	Ajna (in English: "Command")	**Life Area**	Intuition
Location	Forehead	**Crystals**	Lapis lazuli, celestite
Affirmation	"I see."	**Flora**	Hydrangea, sweet pea

Throat Chakra

Sanskrit	Vishuddha (in English: "Purest")	**Life Area**	Communication
Location	Throat	**Crystals**	Sodalite, turquoise
Affirmation	"I speak."	**Flora**	Bluebells, hyacinth

Heart Chakra

Sanskrit	Anahata (in English: "Unstruck")	**Life Area**	Interpersonal connections and relationships
Location	Heart	**Crystals**	Prehnite, rose quartz
Affirmation	"I love."	**Flora**	Lavender, geranium

Solar Plexus Chakra

Sanskrit	Manipura (in English: "Jewel City")	Life Area	Willpower
Location	Naval	Crystals	Tiger's eye, red zircon
Affirmation	"I do."	Flora	Lemon, sunflower

Sacral Chakra

Sanskrit	Svadhishthana (in English: "Where the Self is Established")	Life Area	Ego
Location	Lower abdomen	Crystals	Carnelian, citrine
Affirmation	"I feel."	Flora	Bergamot, orange

Root Chakra

Sanskrit	Muladhara (in English: "Root")	Life Area	Sexuality, survival
Location	Base of spine	Crystals	Bloodstone, garnet
Affirmation	"I am."	Flora	Cedar, pine needles

Spell Jars for the Modern Witch

Major Arcana Tarot Card Associations

0 The Fool

Element	Air
Upright Keywords	Innocence, naivety, new beginnings
Reversed Keywords	Lack of forethought, unnecessary risk-taking

I The Magician

Element	Air
Upright Keywords	Creation, manifestation, willpower
Reversed Keywords	Aimlessness, latent potential

II The High Priestess

Element	Water
Upright Keywords	Psychic perception, inner truth, intuition
Reversed Keywords	Lack of clarity, repressed emotions

III The Empress

Element	Earth
Upright Keywords	Abundance, beauty, caretaker energy, nature
Reversed Keywords	A lack of independence, smothering behavior

IV The Emperor

Element	Fire
Upright Keywords	Authority, control
Reversed Keywords	Rigidity, tyranny

V The Hierophant

Element	Earth
Upright Keywords	Conformity, hierarchies, tradition
Reversed Keywords	Individuality, nonconformity, rebellion

VI The Lovers

Element	Air
Upright Keywords	Crossroads, harmonious unions
Reversed Keywords	Disharmony, parting ways

VII The Chariot

Element	Water
Upright Keywords	Drive, self-control, willpower
Reversed Keywords	Aimlessness, lack of ambition or self-control

VIII Strength

Element	Fire
Upright Keywords	Bravery, compassion, inner strength
Reversed Keywords	Lack of confidence, weakness

IX The Hermit

Element	Earth
Upright Keywords	Contemplation, searching for truth, solitude
Reversed Keywords	Loneliness, isolation

X Wheel of Fortune

Element	Fire
Upright Keywords	Change, cycles, fate
Reversed Keywords	Bad luck, loss of control

XI Justice

Element	Air
Upright Keywords	Cause and effect, consequences, fairness
Reversed Keywords	Lack of personal accountability or responsibility, dishonesty

XII The Hanged Man

Element	Water
Upright Keywords	New perspectives, pause, personal sacrifice
Reversed Keywords	Delays, martyrdom, stalling

XIII Death

Element	Water
Upright Keywords	Transitions, transformations
Reversed Keywords	Resisting change, stagnation

XIV Temperance

Element	Fire
Upright Keywords	Balance, moderation, patience
Reversed Keywords	Lack of balance, extremes, unhealthy excess or restriction

XV The Devil

Element	Earth
Upright Keywords	Feeling powerless or trapped, materialism
Reversed Keywords	Breaking free, restoring balance and self-control

XVI The Tower

Element	Fire
Upright Keywords	Collapse, destruction, unexpected upheaval
Reversed Keywords	Inner transformation, narrowly avoiding catastrophe

XVII The Star

Element	Air
Upright Keywords	Hope, faith, renewal, optimism
Reversed Keywords	Insecurity, hopelessness

XVIII The Moon

Element	Water
Upright Keywords	Illusions, intuition
Reversed Keywords	Confusion, fear, miscommunications

XIX The Sun

Element	Fire
Upright Keywords	Joy, celebration, success
Reversed Keywords	Sadness, negativity, unsuccessful outcomes

XX Judgment

Element	Fire
Upright Keywords	Atonement, reckoning
Reversed Keywords	A lack of self-confidence, ignoring important messages and signs

Helpful Correspondences and Associations

XXI The World

Element	Earth
Upright Keywords	Completion, personal fulfillment, legacy
Reversed Keywords	Lack of closure, feeling personally unfulfilled

Astrological Correspondences

Aries (March 21 – April 20)

Glyph	♈	Planetary Ruler	Mars
Element	Fire	Symbol	Ram
Color	Red	Gemstone	Diamond
Metal	Iron	Tarot Card	The Emperor
Flora	Honeysuckle, peppermint		

Taurus (April 21 – May 20)

Glyph	♉	Planetary Ruler	Venus
Element	Earth	Symbol	Bull
Color	Earthy green, brown	Gemstone	Emerald
Metal	Copper	Tarot Card	The Hierophant
Flora	Poppy, violet		

Gemini (May 21 – June 20)

Glyph		**Planetary Ruler**	Mercury
Element	Air	**Symbol**	Twins
Color	Bright blue, yellow	**Gemstone**	Agate
Metal	Mercury	**Tarot Card**	The Lovers
Flora	Chrysanthemum, lavender		

Cancer (June 21 – July 20)

Glyph		**Planetary Ruler**	Moon
Element	Water	**Symbol**	Crab
Color	Gray, silver	**Gemstone**	Pearl
Metal	Silver	**Tarot Card**	The Chariot
Flora	Southern magnolia, white rose		

Leo (July 21 – August 20)

Glyph		**Planetary Ruler**	Sun
Element	Fire	**Symbol**	Lion
Color	Gold, orange, red	**Gemstone**	Ruby
Metal	Gold	**Tarot Card**	Strength
Flora	Marigold, sunflower		

Virgo (August 21 – September 20)

Glyph	♍	**Planetary Ruler**	Mercury
Element	Earth	**Symbol**	Maiden
Color	Dark brown, navy	**Gemstone**	Carnelian
Metal	Nickel	**Tarot Card**	The Hermit
Flora	Buttercup, eucalyptus		

Libra (September 21 – October 20)

Glyph	♎	**Planetary Ruler**	Venus
Element	Air	**Symbol**	Scales
Color	Pastel pink	**Gemstone**	Chrysoprase
Metal	Copper	**Tarot Card**	Justice
Flora	Daisy, rose		

Scorpio (October 21 – November 20)

Glyph	♏	**Planetary Ruler**	Pluto
Element	Water	**Symbol**	Scorpion
Color	Black, dark red	**Gemstone**	Opal
Metal	Iron	**Tarot Card**	Death
Flora	Gardenia, geranium		

Spell Jars for the Modern Witch

Sagittarius (November 21 – December 20)

Glyph	♐	Planetary Ruler	Jupiter
Element	Fire	Symbol	Centaur, archer
Color	Royal purple	Gemstone	Turquoise
Metal	Tin	Tarot Card	Temperance
Flora	Carnation, dandelion		

Capricorn (December 21 – January 20)

Glyph	♑	Planetary Ruler	Saturn
Element	Earth	Symbol	Sea goat
Color	Blue-gray	Gemstone	Garnet
Metal	Silver	Tarot Card	The Devil
Flora	Pansy, ivy		

Aquarius (January 21 – February 20)

Glyph	♒	Planetary Ruler	Uranus
Element	Air	Symbol	Water bearer
Color	Blue-green	Gemstone	Amethyst
Metal	Aluminum	Tarot Card	The Star
Flora	Goldenrod, orchid		

Pisces (February 21 – March 20)

Glyph	♓	**Planetary Ruler**	Neptune
Element	Water	**Symbol**	Two fish
Color	Sea green	**Gemstone**	Aquamarine
Metal	Platinum	**Tarot Card**	The Moon
Flora	Lilac, lily		

Timing the Spell

Seasonal Associations

SPRING

Best for Spells Relating to	Celebration of milestones, friendship, love
Crystals	Aquamarine, moonstone
Colors	Kelly green, pastels, white
Flora	Honeysuckle, primrose, tulips
Foods	Cheese, chocolate, sprouts

SUMMER

Best for Spells Relating to	Community, personal freedom, joy
Crystals	Tiger's eye, peridot, ruby
Colors	Gold, sky blue, yellow, white
Flora	Dandelion, lemon, saffron
Foods	Fresh fruits, bright citrus flavors

AUTUMN

Best for Spells Relating to	Harvesting the fruits of your hard work, gratitude
Crystals	Howlite, labradorite, smoky quartz
Colors	Earthy greens, gold, burnt orange, rusty reds

Flora	Acorns, fallen leaves, cinnamon
Foods	Pomegranate, gourds, root vegetables

WINTER

Best for Spells Relating to	Guidance, planning for the future
Crystals	Black obsidian, garnet, rose quartz
Colors	Deep green, light cream tones, silver, warm reds
Flora	Holly, mistletoe, pine needles, pinecones
Foods	Dried fruits, mushrooms, roasted nuts

The Full Moons

JANUARY

Sometimes Known as	Wolf Moon
Colors	Gray, white, purple
Best for Magick Relating to	Healing, new beginnings

FEBRUARY

Sometimes Known as	Snow Moon
Colors	Blue, black
Best for Magick Relating to	Planning for the future, purification

MARCH

Sometimes Known as	Worm Moon
Colors	Green, white
Best for Magick Relating to	Abundance, prosperity, technology

APRIL

Sometimes Known as	Pink Moon
Colors	Light green, pink
Best for Magick Relating to	Growth, love, travel

Helpful Correspondences and Associations

MAY

Sometimes Known as	Flower or Planting Moon
Colors	Green, brown
Best for Magick Relating to	Love, overall well-being

JUNE

Sometimes Known as	Strawberry Moon
Colors	Orange, yellow
Best for Magick Relating to	Decision-making, protection

JULY

Sometimes Known as	Thunder Moon
Colors	Green, orange, yellow
Best for Magick Relating to	Cleansing, grounding

AUGUST

Sometimes Known as	Sturgeon or Grain Moon
Colors	Brown, dark green
Best for Magick Relating to	Giving, gratitude

SEPTEMBER

Sometimes Known as	Harvest Moon
Colors	Brown, burnt orange
Best for Magick Relating to	Completion, household magick

OCTOBER

Sometimes Known as	Hunter's or Blood Moon
Colors	Black, orange
Best for Magick Relating to	Ancestral work, finances, the home

NOVEMBER

Sometimes Known as	Beaver Moon
Colors	Blue, green, silver
Best for Magick Relating to	Endurance, perseverance, protection

DECEMBER

Sometimes Known As	Cold Moon
Colors	Black, green, silver
Best for Magick Relating to	Dedication, initiation, renewal

BLUE MOON

A blue moon only happens once every two-and-a-half years or so. It's the second full moon in one month and occurs because the twelve full moons don't divide evenly throughout the calendar year.

Colors	Beige, navy
Best for Magick Relating to	Knowledge, logic, wisdom

Lunar Phase Correspondences

NEW MOON

Tarot Card	The Fool
Best for Magick Relating to	New beginnings, self-improvement, setting intentions

WAXING CRESCENT

Tarot Card	The Magician
Best for Magick Relating to	Luck, prosperity

FIRST QUARTER

Tarot Card	Strength
Best for Magick Relating to	Growth, learning, transformation

WAXING GIBBOUS

Tarot Card	The Star
Best for Magick Relating to	Aspirations, endurance, patience

FULL MOON

Tarot Card	The Sun
Best for Magick Relating to	Achieving goals, fulfillment, gratitude

WANING GIBBOUS

Tarot Card	The Tower
Best for Magick Relating to	Banishing negativity, cutting ties, reaping the rewards of hard work

LAST QUARTER

Tarot Card	Judgment
Best for Magick Relating to	Introspection, letting go, release

WANING CRESCENT

Tarot Card	Justice
Best for Magick Relating to	Atonement, divination, reflection

Days of the Week Correspondences

SUNDAY

Ruler	The Sun
Metal	Gold
Colors	Pink, orange, yellow
Crystals	Amber, sunstone
Flora	Cinnamon, sunflowers
Best for Magick Relating to	Creativity, new beginnings

MONDAY

Ruler	The Moon
Metal	Silver
Colors	Pastel blue, white, silver
Crystals	Moonstone, opal
Flora	Chamomile, mint, willow
Best for Magick Relating to	The Moon, intuition, seeking guidance

TUESDAY

Ruler	Mars
Metal	Iron

Spell Jars for the Modern Witch

Colors	Black, orange, scarlet red
Crystals	Garnet, ruby
Flora	Coneflower, thistle
Best for Magick Relating to	Conflict, staking claim, unions

WEDNESDAY

Ruler	Mercury
Metal	Zinc
Colors	Shades of green
Crystals	Green aventurine, green jade
Flora	Ferns, lavender
Best for Magick Relating to	Collaborations, communication, interpersonal relationships

THURSDAY

Ruler	Jupiter
Metal	Tin
Colors	Purple, royal blue
Crystals	Amethyst, emerald
Flora	Alfalfa, coriander
Best for Magick Relating to	Family, legacy, prosperity

FRIDAY

Ruler	Venus
Metal	Copper
Colors	Light blue, pink
Crystals	Malachite, rose quartz
Flora	Rosemary, roses, vanilla
Best for Magick Relating to	Harmony, friendship, love

SATURDAY

Ruler	Saturn
Metal	Pewter

Colors	Dark shades, especially dark purple
Crystals	Black obsidian, jet
Flora	Mullein, thyme
Best for Magick Relating to	Banishing negativity, protection

Times of the Day Correspondences

DAWN

Best for Magick Relating to	Hope, new beginnings, renewal

MORNING

Best for Magick Relating to	Clarity, taking charge, the present

NOON

Best for Magick Relating to	Fairness, justice, logic

DUSK

Best for Magick Relating to	Closure, endings

NIGHT

Best for Magick Relating to	Contemplation, introspection, rest, solitude

MIDNIGHT

Considered the most potent hour for magick.

Best for Magick Relating to	Astral projection, psychic perception

Crystals

Crystal Shapes and Their Uses

Carved Crystals	Invoke the symbolism of the shape into which they're carved. Common shapes include animals, angels, and hearts.
Chips	Often used in spell jars or put into wearable vials for jewelry; sometimes used as supporting crystals in crystal grids.
Crystal Cluster	Radiates the crystal's energy throughout a space.

Spell Jars for the Modern Witch

Cubes	Gives off grounding energy, holds intentions, and provides a connection to the physical realm.
Double-Terminated	Absorbs and transfers the crystal's energy.
Egg	Emits energy evenly and symbolizes fertility. (This doesn't just refer to pregnancy, but also relates to the idea of being fertile with new ideas, creativity, and/or hope.)
Palmstone	Facilitates the transfer of personal energy.
Point	Directs energy, sending the energy in the direction of the point.
Pyramids	Transmits and generates energy. Often used as the anchoring crystal in the center of crystal grids.
Raw	A general-purpose shape that gives off unfocused energy. Often used as the main stones and crystals surrounding the anchor in crystal grids.
Sphere	Emits energy evenly in all directions. Used in divination practices, such as scrying.
Tumbled:	An accessible form of crystal that gives off gentle, consistent energy.

Crystal Index

Amethyst	Balances emotions, relieves stress, used in dream and sleep magick
Azurite	Enhances clarity and psychic perception
Black Kyanite	Banishes negative energy, enhances psychic perception
Black Obsidian	Banishes negativity, provides spiritual protection, promotes optimism
Black Onyx	Provides spiritual protection, inspires inner strength
Black Tourmaline	Banishes negativity, provides spiritual protection
Bloodstone	Manifests courage, promotes longevity
Blue Apatite	Enhances psychic perception, opens channels to higher realms and the divine

Helpful Correspondences and Associations

Blue Chalcedony	Promotes clarity, opens channels for communication, reveals truth
Blue Kyanite	Promotes communication and honesty
Blue Lace Agate	Promotes justice
Carnelian	Energizes, inspires passion, stimulates creativity
Celestite	Enhances intuition, promotes divine communication
Chrysocolla	Enhances clarity, uncovers the truth
Citrine	Promotes positivity, inspires optimism
Clear Quartz	Amplifies, enhances, and directs energy and magick
Crazy Lace Agate	Inspires lightheartedness and happiness
Dalmatian Jasper	Promotes playfulness, aids in keeping a healthy, balanced perspective
Dendritic Agate	Provides grounding, stabilizes emotions
Emerald	Promotes good luck, inspires love, encourages success
Garnet	Enhances courage and fortitude
Green Aventurine	Promotes emotional healing, used in garden magick
Green Jade	Attracts good luck, promotes harmony, inspires love
Hematite	Promotes grounding and spiritual protection
Howlite	Opens communication; often used in past life spellwork and ancestor magick
Jet	Builds connections to the past, provides grounding, promotes spiritual protection
Kambaba Jasper	Aids in accepting changes, promotes calm energy and peace
Labradorite	Provides spiritual protection, promotes courage and strength; great for empaths
Lapis Lazuli	Promotes learning, enhances wisdom
Malachite	Enhances courage, promotes inner stability and strength during times of transition

Spell Jars for the Modern Witch

Mookaite Jasper	Enhances courage, inspires self-reliance
Moonstone	Promotes emotional balance and healing, calms the mind, enhances clarity and psychic perception
Morganite	Promotes harmony and love
Moss Agate	Enhances connection with nature, provides grounding, promotes personal growth
Nuummite	Enhances psychic awareness, strengthens personal magick
Opal	Inspires happiness, attracts good luck
Prehnite	Promotes emotional balance
Pyrite	Attracts good luck, promotes success; used in money magick
Rainbow Fluorite	Promotes emotional balance, inspires a sense of inner peace; used in dream and sleep magick
Red Aragonite	Inspires creativity and passion, energizes, builds self-confidence, promotes self-reliance
Red Zircon	Energizes, removes energetic blockages, stimulates ambition and focus
Rose Quartz	Balances emotions, promotes harmony
Ruby	Attracts prosperity, inspires courage
Sapphire	Brings wisdom, enhances memory
Selenite	Cleanses and purifies
Shungite	Absorbs negative energy, protects against electromagnetic frequencies
Smoky Quartz	Stabilizes emotions and chaotic energy
Sodalite	Facilitates easy and effective communication, helps build the self-confidence needed for self-expression
Sugilite	Promotes clarity and truth, promotes grace in times of distress
Sunstone	Promotes warm emotional connections, inspires happiness
Turquoise	Attracts friendship, enhances personal power, provides spiritual protection
Vanadinite	Inspires action, promotes creativity and focus

Helpful Correspondences and Associations

Flowers, Herbs, and Other Natural Ingredients Index

Natural Ingredients Index

Acorn	Attracts good luck, especially on journeys
Alfalfa	Attracts prosperity and financial success, promotes a happy home
Allspice	Brings success and financial prosperity
Almond	Promotes knowledge, inspires self-reliance
Angelica	Provides spiritual protection
Apple	Promotes harmony and success within relationships; used in garden magick
Ash	Attracts good luck, promotes prosperity
Basil	Attracts good luck, promotes love and understanding, provides spiritual protection
Bay Leaf	Provides spiritual protection, promotes success; used in spiritual cleansing
Bergamot	Attracts financial success, promotes peaceful sleep
Blackberry Leaf	Attracts prosperity, provides spiritual protection
Black Pepper	Provides protection from negativity; used in banishment spells
Blueberry	Promotes happiness; used in magick involving children
Cardamom	Promotes passion, inspires fidelity
Carnation	Encourages emotional balance, promotes inner strength
Catnip	Inspires happiness, attracts good luck; used in animal magick
Cedar	Attracts luck, provides spiritual protection
Chamomile	Calms anxiety, reduces stress, promotes peaceful sleep
Chickweed	Balances emotions, promotes love; used in animal magick and lunar spellwork

Spell Jars for the Modern Witch

Chili	Inspires passion, provides protection; used in banishment spells
Cinnamon	Promotes swift success; used in solar spellwork
Clove	Opens psychic connections, provides protection from negativity; used in divination
Coffee	Clears energetic blockages, helps in setting boundaries, speeds up results
Coriander	Promotes peace and protection, especially for the home
Cumin	Inspires passion; used in love spells
Cypress	Aids in making peace with death or loss; used in mourning spellwork
Evening Primrose	Attracts love, promotes peace; used in lunar spellwork
Honey	Attracts good luck, promotes comfort; sweetens spellwork
Juniper	Brings clarity; used in spiritual cleansing
Lavender	Promotes calm and peace; often used in dream and sleep magick
Lemon	Energizes the senses, moves stagnant energy, clears energetic blockages
Lemongrass	Spiritually cleanses personal energy to enhance psychic perception
Marigold	Inspires happiness; used in spells seeking fairness and justice
Moss	Grounds, settles chaotic energy, soothes hurt feelings
Mullein	Wards off nightmares and negative entities; often used in spells regarding transitions or travel to promote courage and offer protection.
Nettle Leaf	Aids during times of acute stress or emergency by enhancing inner strength, quick-thinking, and sensible decisions
Orange	Inspires swift action, promotes happiness
Passionflower	Attracts friendship and love
Peach Pit	Brings comfort; offers spiritual protection

Helpful Correspondences and Associations

Peppermint	Clears negative energy in a space, attracts higher vibrations; used in purification and healing spells
Pine Needles	Provides protection and purification; used in banishment spells
Poplar	Facilitates communication, soothes hurt feelings
Pumpkin Seeds	Promotes harmony and happiness at home and within families, clears negative energy and attracts positive, high-vibe energy in its place
Raspberry Leaf	Calms emotions, provides clarity
Red Clover	Promotes healthy, equal, passionate relationships
Rosemary	Wards off negativity, enhances memory, promotes nostalgia and faithfulness; often used in love spells (Rosemary is traditionally used in bridal bouquets.)
Roses	Attracts friendship, inspires happiness, promotes passion
Sage	Banishes negativity; used in purification spellwork
Sea Salt	Provides protection; used in spiritual cleansing
St. John's Wort	Promotes prophetic dreams and protects against hexes and curses
Sunflower	Inspires happiness, longevity, and vitality
Sweetgrass	Attracts positivity; often used in smoke cleansing
Thistle	Enhances clarity and psychic perception; used in spiritual cleansing
Thyme	Promotes courage, offers protection from nightmares; used in beauty and self-care magick
Vanilla	Provides comfort, promotes emotional security, encourages warm feelings, attracts loving connections
Willow	Promotes peace, provides spiritual protection; often used in lunar magick
Yarrow	Attracts love, promotes confidence; often used in love spells and marriage rites

Spell Jars for the Modern Witch

Essential Oils Commonly Used in Spellwork Index

Many people use essential oils in their daily lives. Some people believe that certain essential oils can heal aches, pains, and other ailments, and many essential oils are known for their mood-boosting properties. This is a list of essential oils commonly used in spellwork. There are many more varieties of essential oils out there! These are the ones I see used most often in spellwork.

Personally, when I choose to incorporate essential oils into a spell jar, I put a couple drops into it as the final step. You can also consider adding a few drops to a cotton ball or cloth, then placing it in the spell jar. Keep in mind that essential oils can degrade certain materials, so be aware of the other ingredients in your spell jars and how the oils may affect them.

Essential Oils Index	
Almond	Promotes good sense, enhances knowledge and wisdom
Bamboo	Promotes good luck and deep relaxation
Basil	Brings clarity and focus
Cedar	Banishes nightmares, offers spiritual protection
Clove	Provides protection from negativity, opens psychic connections
Eucalyptus	Provides spiritual protection, promotes overall well-being
Frankincense	Enhances intuition and a connection with the divine; used in purification spells
Hibiscus	Attracts friendship, promotes love

Jasmine	Promotes astral projection and prophetic dreams; used in spellwork involving sleep
Juniper	Provides purification, offers spiritual protection
Lavender	Promotes a calm mental state, encourages relaxation, softens emotions
Lemongrass	Enhances focus and mental energy, opens psychic connections
Orange	Promotes quick action and energy; used in prosperity spellwork
Patchouli	Helps to reconnect you with your true self and potential, attracts prosperity
Peppermint	Clears negativity, promotes focus and quick thinking
Pine	Provides protection from negative energy; often used in spellwork involving the home
Rosemary	Enhances memory, promotes nostalgia; used in love and union spellwork
Sage	Provides spiritual protection; used in purification spellwork and smoke cleansing
Vanilla	Attracts abundance, enhances comfort

Magickal Tools Index

There are many items and objects that can be used in modern magickal practices. These are the fundamental tools you should familiarize yourself with and consider incorporating into your own spellcasting practices. Keep in mind there are many other culturally and religiously specific tools used in witchcraft and spiritual crafts and rites.

Magickal Tools Index

Athame	A ritual knife or dagger used to direct energy and carve symbols or words into objects, such as candles, during spellwork. They can be made from crystal, metal, or wood.
Bells, chimes, and singing bowls	Used to send energetically purifying vibrations throughout a space. They honor and invoke the element Air.
Besom	Besoms, also known as brooms, are used to ritualistically sweep away stagnant and negative energy.
Candle	Candles honor and invoke the element Fire and are used to attract energy and hold intent. Some people dress candles in sacred oils and herbs during spellwork. They can be carved with symbols or words to hold specific intent during rituals. Many believe that the color of the candle affects the type of energy it attracts. See page 49 for the table of Color Correspondences.
Cauldron	Cast-iron cauldrons can be used to brew potions and tinctures, hold Full Moon Water, or safely burn ritual candles and incense.
Censer	Censers hold incense that is burned for ritualistic purposes.
Chalice	Chalices honor and invoke the element Water. They can hold Full Moon Water, sacred tinctures, or potions. Often during coven meetings, members pass around and drink from a sacred chalice as a unity rite.
Pendulum	There are so many divination tools in the world of spirituality and witchcraft, but pendulums are one of the most common.
Pentacle	Pentacles honor and invoke the element Earth. They represent protection and life aspects relating to the material realm, such as the home and finances.
Wand	Wands are used to direct magick and energy. They can be made from crystals, metal, or wood. They're most commonly associated with the element Fire, though some traditions associate them with Air.

Part 2

Spell Jar Recipes

*N*ow, to dive into the creation of spell jars! You'll see a lack of listed quantities throughout these spells. That's because the quantities of ingredients are up to you! You'll have to consider the amounts you have on hand, along with the size of your selected jar. For example, the amount of crystals you'd use in a tiny spell jar necklace vial is small compared to the amount you'd use in a mason spell jar. Feel free to experiment with different forms of the crystals listed in these spells, as well. For example, if a spell calls for rose quartz, you can use tiny rose quartz chips, tumbles, or larger carved specimens. Where natural ingredients are listed, it's up to you as the spellcaster to choose whether to use dried or fresh versions of the ingredients. I like to use fresh ingredients whenever possible, unless I'm creating a long-term spell jar that I want to stand the test of time. Then, I'll often opt to use dried ingredients, as they're more stable and long-lasting. The beauty of spellwork is that it's so customizable. Use these spells as a guide, but remember that you're allowed to deviate from them in any way your intuition guides you.

Spell Jar Recipes

Spell Jars for Your Home

Cultivate a Stable, Happy Home Life

We all want peaceful, happy homes, but that often takes work! I created this spell jar to help facilitate ease within family dynamics. Every member of our families has their own unique personality and communication styles, so it makes sense that great communication and healthy self-expression are essential to a functional, happy home life. The stability of the IV of Wands tarot card is enhanced by crystals and flora that have been carefully curated to promote happy energy at home.

- ✳ Paper, brown or green preferred
- ✳ Writing tool, brown or green preferred
- ✳ 1 or 2 drops lavender essential oil
- ✳ IV of Wands tarot card
- ✳ Alfalfa
- ✳ Coriander
- ✳ Pumpkin seeds
- ✳ Grounding crystals and crystals that promote healthy communication, such as black kyanite, blue kyanite, smoky quartz, and sodalite

1. On the paper, write an affirmation relating to the goal of the spell jar, such as, "This is a happy home. My family is communicative, healthy, and stable."

2. Anoint your written affirmation with a drop or two of lavender essential oil and add it to the spell jar.

3. Add the IV of Wands tarot card to the spell jar.

4. Sprinkle in alfalfa, coriander, and pumpkin seeds.

5. Add the black kyanite, blue kyanite, smoky quartz, and sodalite to the jar.

6. Seal the spell jar using the method of your choice.

7. To activate the spell, create energetic momentum by gently shaking it.

Keep this spell jar somewhere central to your home life. For example, if your family has a place in your home where everyone congregates regularly, such as a dining room, living room, or home theater, keep the spell jar there.

For a Healthy, Prosperous Garden

Calling all gardeners! Whether you're already rocking a green thumb or you're looking for a little boost in the plant-parenting department, this spell jar is for you. Balance is the key to gardening; plants need just the right mixture of sunlight and water to thrive. This spell jar is designed to promote balance and nurturing within your garden or among your potted plants.

* Green candle
* Your preferred lighting tool, such as matches or a lighter
* Paper, green or brown colors preferred
* Writing tool, green or brown colors preferred
* Enough dirt from your garden to fill ⅓ of your jar
* Dried apple
* Orange peel (fresh or dried)
* Lemon balm
* Aventurine
* Moss agate

Spell Jars for Your Home

1. Light the green candle. While either closing your eyes to concentrate or watching the flame, visualize plants growing and thriving. Picture happy, healthy plants worthy of winning a Best Bloom contest.

2. On the paper, write your garden goals in an affirmative way, such as, "This flora is nurtured, healthy, balanced, and bountiful." Add these affirmations to the spell jar.

3. Pour the dirt into the bottom of the jar.

4. Add the dried apple, orange peel, and lemon balm to the jar.

5. Add the green aventurine and moss agate on top.

6. Seal the jar using your chosen method.

7. To activate the spell, bury the spell jar in earth for 24 hours.

You can either keep the spell jar buried in your garden or plant pot, or place it somewhere near your potted plants where it won't be disturbed.

New Home Blessing

Congratulations on your new home! Whether you've just signed the lease on a new apartment, bought a new house, or are moving into a new room in a shared living situation, this New Home Blessing spell jar is designed to purify and refresh the space while filling it with all the good vibes you need to start this new chapter off on the right foot.

- ✳ Compass
- ✳ 4 protective crystals or stones, such as black kyanite, black tourmaline, jet, and obsidian (see notes)
- ✳ Paper, black and white colors preferred
- ✳ Writing tool, black and white colors preferred
- ✳ Selenite
- ✳ X of Cups tarot card
- ✳ Dirt from your garden, or from somewhere just outside your home
- ✳ Alfalfa
- ✳ Carnation
- ✳ Sunflower seeds
- ✳ Thistle
- ✳ Sea salt

1. Use the compass to find the cardinal directions. With the jar in the center, place your four protective crystals just outside of the jar in each of the cardinal directions.

2. While visualizing your home filling with a protective, powerful glow, write a protective affirmation, such as, "My home is cleansed, purified, divinely protected, and full of love."

3. Hold the selenite in both of your hands and recite your affirmation aloud.

4. Add the written affirmation to the jar.

5. Place the X of Cups tarot card into the jar.

6. Sprinkle in the dirt.

7. Add the alfalfa, carnation, sunflower seeds, and thistle to the jar. Then add the sea salt on top.

8. Gather the four protective crystals and add them to the jar, along with the selenite.

9. Seal the spell jar using the method of your choice.

10. Activate the spell by gently tapping the jar with your finger or preferred magickal tool while envisioning your new home radiating happy, positive magickal energy.

Keep your spell jar in a central place in your home, or by the main entrance to your home. Make sure it's placed somewhere where it won't be disturbed. Charge it on every full moon to refresh its power.

Notes: All four of your protective crystals can be the same type a mix.

Spell Jars for Interpersonal Relationships

Attract Attention (Stand Out and Be Noticed)

Have you been feeling like a bit of a wallflower lately? Whether you're looking to attract the attention of someone specific or a certain group of people, or you're just plain ol' ready for your time to flourish in the spotlight, this spell jar is intended to help you stand out and get noticed. Shine on, darling!

* Red or pink candle (see notes)
* Your preferred lighting tool, such as matches or a lighter
* Paper, bright colors preferred
* Writing tool, bright colors preferred
* 1 to 2 drops orange essential oil
* Queen of Wands tarot card (see notes)
* Crystals to stimulate energy, positivity, and vitality, such as carnelian, citrine, red zircon, and sunstone
* Cardamom
* Catnip
* Passionflower
* Rose petals (see notes)
* Yarrow
* Colorful confetti (see notes)

1. Light your candle.

2. On the paper, write an affirmation or two relating to the goal of your spell. For example, if I were creating this spell jar to manifest confidence and command the spotlight during a party that has major potential for new friendships and even romance, I might write, "I am attractive, effervescent, and magnetic. No longer a wallflower, I am the radiant life of the party. Positive new connections are drawn to me like a moth to flame."

3. Speak the written affirmations aloud. Repeat them until you believe them!

4. Place a drop or two of orange essential oil onto your written affirmations to activate and amplify their magickal intent.

5. Fold the written affirmations and add them to the jar.

6. Add the Queen of Wands tarot card to the spell jar. As you're doing this, visualize your goal coming true.

7. Add the chosen crystals to the spell jar.

8. Add the cardamom, catnip, passionflower, rose petals, and yarrow.

9. Sprinkle the confetti into the jar.

10. Seal the jar using your preferred method.

11. Activate the spell jar by charging it in sunlight for an hour.

Whenever it needs to be refreshed, place it in sunlight, or add another drop or two of the invigorating orange essential oil to the jar.

Notes:

CANDLES: Use a red candle if you want to attract romantic love; opt for pink if you want to attract new friendships or are making a general attraction spell.

TAROT CARD: The Queen of Wands tarot card represents someone who's vivacious, attractive, creative, and a social butterfly. Using this tarot card in this spell jar will help to imbue it with the magnetic, effervescent energy of the Queen of Wands.

ROSE PETALS: Use red rose petals to attract romantic love; use pink or yellow to attract friendship or for general attraction.

CONFETTI: I like to use metallic confetti because it has the added bonus of being reflective, which draws extra attention. Choose a type of confetti that's bright, bold, glittery, and/or metallic.

Reconnect with a Loved One

Have you lost touch with an old friend you grew apart from? Are you missing the close connection you once had with a now-distant family member? Perhaps you're longing for a former romantic connection that could still have unfinished business. This spell jar has been created to help rebuild an energetic and magickal connection between you and the loved one on your mind. Bear in mind that this spell jar isn't a guarantee that the subject of the spell will come back into your life. Ultimately, what becomes of the magickal connection built with this spell is decided by you and the other person. Keep your own magickal ethics and the subject's boundaries in mind when deciding whether or not to create this spell jar. But I've used this recipe personally to help reconnect with a close friend I'd drifted away from and missed, and I'm convinced it helped facilitate our reunion and the rekindling of our bestie-ship!

* Paper, blue or green preferred
* Writing tool, blue or green preferred
* 1 to 2 drops pure vanilla extract, or vanilla essential oil
* Object that represents the loved one you're looking to reconnect with (see notes)
* Crystals for emotional healing and building connections, such as blue chalcedony, emerald, green aventurine, moonstone, morganite, and prehnite
* Alfalfa
* Basil
* Carnation
* Dried apple slices
* Red clover
* Rosemary

1. On the paper, write an affirmation or message that both addresses the subject of the spell and relates to the goal of the spell. For example, if I'm looking to reconnect with a family

member with whom I've had a falling out, I might address the message to the family member by writing, "Aunt Marie, it's time to bury the hatchet and reconnect. I miss having you in my life. I miss your laughter, your wise advice, and your award-winning blueberry cobbler. I want to reconnect."

2. Speak the written message aloud.

3. Add a drop or two of your vanilla ingredient to the written message, then place the message into the spell jar.

4. Add your chosen object that represents the subject of the spell.

5. Add the gathered crystals to the spell jar.

6. Add the alfalfa, basil, carnation, dried apples slices, red clover, and rosemary to the spell jar.

7. Seal the jar using your preferred method.

8. Activate this spell jar by keeping it in the moonlight for a full night.

While this spell jar alone may not compel the subject to contact you, it will put you on their mind and help energetically facilitate the restoration of a connection. Ultimately, both parties have to be willing. This spell jar helps to promote the peace, nostalgia, and healing needed for reconnection.

Notes: Objects that represent your loved ones can be a charm featuring their zodiac sign, a flower or trinket that reminds you of them, a photo of them, or even just their name written on a piece of paper.

Stop Gossip

By now, I think we all have had some experience with gossip in our lives. Whether the tittle-tattle has involved scandalous rumors, hurtful untruths, or spreading someone else's personal, private information, we all know just how harmful and toxic gossip can be. If you're having problems with behind-your-back whispers and the great, proverbial rumor mill, this spell jar will help to stop that unproductive chatter. After all, doesn't everyone have better things to do?

* A candle, black preferred
* Your preferred lighting tool, such as matches or a lighter
* Paper, black preferred
* Writing tool, black preferred
* Small piece of string or yarn (enough to tie up in at least a few knots), black or red colors preferred
* Sharp object, such as a sewing needle or push pin
* Crystals to protect against negativity, such as black kyanite, black obsidian, black onyx, black tourmaline, hematite, and shungite
* Black pepper
* Cloves
* Frankincense
* Pine needles
* St. John's Wort

1. Light the candle.

2. On the piece of paper, write an affirmation relating to the goal of your spell, such as, "No gossip about me or slander against me propagates. Tongues wag about me no longer."

3. Speak the written affirmation aloud.

4. Place the written affirmation into the spell jar.

5. Take hold of your selected string or yarn and knot it several times. This represents a wagging tongue being silenced. Each knot stops the trail of gossip from spreading further.

6. Push your chosen sharp object into the knotted string to activate the spell, and place this into the spell jar.

7. Add the gathered crystals to the spell jar.

8. Sprinkle in the black pepper, cloves, frankincense, pine needles, and St. John's Wort.

9. Seal the jar using your preferred method.

10. To activate the spell jar, bury it at the far edge of your property.

If you're unable to bury it in the ground, I recommend sealing it tightly and keeping it hidden somewhere it won't be stumbled upon or disturbed, such as a dark, hidden space in a basement. Many people believe that spell jars like this are only effective as long as they remain hidden, so make an effort to keep it private and out of sight.

Spell Jars for Transitions

Accept Change and Transitions

Let's face it: change can be difficult to accept. If you find yourself fearing transitions or digging your heels in and refusing to meet them head-on, this spell jar is for you. It's designed to bring you comfort on this next journey, giving you the inner strength and divine guidance you need to meet challenges and changes with grace.

✳ Black or white candle

✳ Your preferred lighting tool, such as matches or a lighter

✳ Paper, black and/or white preferred

✳ Writing tool, black and/or white preferred

✳ Death tarot card

✳ Crystals to help manifest inner strength, enhance your psychic awareness to help open you to divine guidance or messages, and promote inner peace, such as blue apatite, chrysocolla, and lapis lazuli

✳ Acorn

✳ Cypress

✳ Mullein

✳ Nettle leaf

1. Light the candle.

2. On the paper, write an affirmation relating to the goal of this spell jar. Be specific. For example, if I were creating this spell jar to help me navigate the stress of moving to a new location, I might write, "I have everything I need to make this move a

success. This move is a very positive next step in the journey of becoming my best self and living my best life."

3. Speak your affirmation aloud. Repeat it, if necessary, until it really resonates with you.

4. Fold the written affirmation and seal it shut with wax from the candle.

5. Add the written affirmation to the spell jar.

6. Add the Death tarot card to the spell jar.

7. Drop in the blue apatite, chrysocolla, and lapis lazuli, or whichever crystals you have chosen for this spell.

8. Add the acorn, cypress, mullein, and nettle leaf to the spell jar.

9. Activate the spell jar by holding it in both hands, so your palms are touching the jar, and visualize magick flowing from you into the jar.

10. Seal the jar using your preferred method.

Keep this spell jar somewhere personal, away from curious eyes, such as a bedside table drawer or jewelry box. Visit the spell jar, hold it in both hands, and meditate with it whenever you feel like you need an extra boost of inner fortitude to get through this transition.

Heal and Move On

Some people just aren't meant to be in our lives forever. People and interpersonal dynamics change over time, and sometimes friendships, relationships, and other connections run their course. These transitions can be emotionally difficult, even if we know deep down that they're for the best. This spell jar is intended to help you heal your heart and move on.

* Bell or chimes
* Green candle
* Your preferred lighting tool, such as matches or a lighter
* Paper, green preferred
* Writing tool, green preferred
* III of Swords tarot card
* Crystals for clearing negativity and soothing emotional wounds, such as black kyanite, emerald, green aventurine, lapis lazuli, and rose quartz

* Carnation
* Chamomile
* Cypress
* Mullein
* Vanilla
* 1 drop peppermint essential oil

1. Ring the bell or play the chimes to clear any stagnant or low vibrational energy from your creation space.

2. Light the green candle.

3. On the paper, write an affirmation relating to the goal of this spell jar. For example, if I were creating this spell jar to help me get over the loss of a close friendship, I might write, "I understand that some people aren't meant to stay in my life forever. I'm grateful for the friendship [my former friend] and

I had but acknowledge that it's run its course. New fulfilling friendships are coming my way."

4. Speak your affirmations aloud.

5. Fold your written affirmations, seal the paper with candle wax, and place the written affirmations in the spell jar.

6. Place the III of Swords tarot card in the spell jar, but be sure it's upside-down in orientation. When reversed, the III of Swords card symbolizes swords falling out of your heart—emotional healing and moving on.

7. Place the black kyanite, emerald, green aventurine, lapis lazuli, and rose quartz or your chosen crystals in the spell jar.

8. Add the carnation, chamomile, cypress, mullein, vanilla, and to the spell jar.

9. Add a drop of peppermint essential oil to the spell jar to activate its magick.

10. Seal the jar using your preferred method.

Hold this spell jar so that both of your palms are touching it whenever you're feeling down about the ending of your friendship, relationship, or other personal connection. Place the crystal selenite on or near the spell jar to refresh and charge it.

Grounding and Stabilization

Life can get busy and hectic. Sometimes, we feel so caught up in regretting the past or focusing on the future that we forget about the present. This spell jar is intended to draw your focus back to the present moment where it truly belongs. This will stabilize your energy and give you the support you need to carry on without being so bothered and swayed by challenges and distractions.

※ Paper, brown preferred

※ Writing tool, brown preferred

※ Enough dirt to fill about ½ of the chosen jar

※ Crystals and stones that stabilize emotions and ground chaotic energy, such as fossils, garnet, hematite, and smoky quartz

1. Sit with both feet flat on the floor. Close your eyes and meditate for a while. Take calm, deep breaths. Notice each of your senses in turn, and what they're perceiving in this very moment. This will help ground you and bring you into the present time.

2. On the paper, write a grounding affirmation, such as, "I am centered, strong, and grounded."

3. Read your affirmation aloud. You can do this once, or chant it until you feel it really resonates with you.

4. Add the written affirmations to the spell jar.

5. Pour your gathered dirt over your written affirmations, burying them in the spell jar.

6. Add the stabilizing crystals to the spell jar.

7. Seal the jar using your preferred method.

8. Activate the spell jar by holding it in both hands, so your palms are touching the jar, and visualize magick flowing from you into the jar.

Consider making a miniature version of this spell jar to wear as jewelry. Use crystal chips to save space. Alternatively, you can carry it with you in a bag, briefcase, pocket, or purse.

Memorialize a Loved One

I designed this spell jar as a precious memorial for a loved one in my life—a little pit bull puppy I'd adopted who was born with a catastrophic disease that she just couldn't beat. I've since made versions of this spell jar for other loved ones who've passed on. It's intended to honor your loved one and bring some peace to your grief.

* White candle
* Your preferred lighting tool, such as matches or a lighter
* Photograph or drawing of the loved one you're memorializing (that you don't mind writing on)
* Writing tool, white or silver preferred
* Paper, if necessary
* Items associated with the loved one you're memorializing (see notes)

* Crystals for comfort, love, and support during transitions, such as amethyst, howlite, malachite, moonstone, and rose quartz
* Chamomile
* Chickweed
* Cypress
* Lavender

Spell Jars for Transitions

1. Light the candle

2. Hold the photograph or drawing of your loved one in both hands. Close your eyes and bring them to the forefront of your mind's eye. Try to incorporate as many of your senses as possible. Remember the sound of their voice; the way their favorite shampoo or perfume smelled; their favorite foods, or any strong, positive food-related memory centered around them; and the feeling of their hugs.

3. When your loved one feels very present in your mind, turn the photo over and write a message to your loved one. It can be as long or short as you want; if you need more room, use a separate sheet of paper when you run out of room on the back of the photo or drawing. Say what you need to say, whether that's as simple as, "Safe travels. I love you," or as complex as profound professions of love and grief.

4. If you used extra paper to write your note, fold it up and seal it with candle wax.

5. Place the photo and writings in the spell jar.

6. Add the items that are associated with your loved one. Take a moment to hold each one and think of your loved one before placing them in individually.

7. Add the amethyst, howlite, malachite, moonstone, and rose quartz, or other chosen crystals, to the spell jar.

8. Add the chamomile, chickweed, cypress, and lavender.

9. Seal the jar using your preferred method.

10. Activate the spell jar by burying it in the ground for at least 24 hours.

If burying the spell jar is not accessible for you, place it in the moonlight overnight, preferably either during the waning crescent lunar phase or a full moon. Keep this spell jar wherever you intuitively feel it should be placed. Personally, I give my memorial spell jars pride of place on the mantle, but you may feel called to keep your spell jar somewhere more private, such as on top of a dresser or high shelf. That's perfectly okay, too.

Notes: For humans, you could consider using baby teeth, a lock of hair, their jewelry, trinkets that remind you of them, and flowers saved from funeral ceremonies. For pets, consider using the animal's fur, discarded feathers, a bit of water from a tank in the case of aquatic animals, or sand from a reptilian habitat.

Success in Buying or Renting a Home

Alright, let's face it: Whether you're renting or buying, finding a new dwelling can be a stressful process. Between location and commute concerns, amenities, parking availability, home inspections, school district research, and pet policies, finding the perfect space that meets all your needs and wants can feel drawn-out and daunting. I created this spell jar recipe to help you manifest a smooth transition into your next home.

* Paper, brown or green preferred

* Writing tool, brown or green preferred

* List of all the qualities your new home must have

* Print-out of new home listing (see notes)

* Charm or small object that represents home to you (see notes)

* **Crystals that promote good luck, easy transitions, and positive vibes, such as black obsidian, dalmatian jasper, green aventurine, kambaba jasper, and malachite**

* **Acorn**
* **Allspice**
* **Mullein**
* **Pumpkin seeds**

1. On the paper, write an affirmation using the list of all your must-have qualities in a new dwelling. For example, I might write, "I will have an easy and smooth transition into my new home. My new home will be in a safe area without any dog breed bans. It will be a solid, safe, historic home with updated electrical system and plumbing, a fenced backyard, and friendly neighbors. So be it."

2. Speak the affirmations aloud.

3. Add the written affirmation to the spell jar. If you have a specific home in mind, add the listing for that home to the spell jar as well.

4. Add to the spell jar the small charm or object that represents home to you.

5. Place obsidian, dalmatian jasper, green aventurine, kambaba jasper, and malachite, or your chosen crystals, in the spell jar.

6. Add the acorn, allspice, mullein, and pumpkin seeds.

7. Seal the spell jar using your preferred method.

8. To activate the spell jar, place it in sunlight to soak up the sun's joyful, warm rays.

Carry this jar in your bag, purse, or pocket when you go to see prospective new homes. To imbue your endeavors with the energy of this spell jar, keep it near you when dealing with any work relating to finding or finalizing a new home purchase or rental, such as making phone calls to agents or researching properties.

Notes:

PRINT-OUT: This is only if you have a specific dwelling in mind that you're looking to manifest success in buying or renting for this spell jar.

CHARM: This can be a small house-shaped charm, a miniature wooden spoon if you love to cook, a little fireplace charm, or, in a pinch, you could simply write the words "home, sweet home" on a piece of paper.

Success in Selling Your Home

Have you ever walked into a building and immediately gotten bad vibes? You can't put your finger on it, but something about the space just makes you uncomfortable. Well, the opposite is possible, too; some places are filled with positive, peaceful energy that makes us feel safe and comfortable as soon as we pass the threshold. The latter is the sort of energy this spell jar is intended to manifest. Our dwellings hold energetic memories and imprints from the lives that have been lived there. My best advice for you is to think of your home as a living being, not just an object. Your time living in this dwelling has come to an end, and this spell jar is created to manifest good luck and financial prosperity during the speedy and efficient sale of your home. It's time to attract new buyers and usher in a new chapter in your home's story.

Spell Jars for Transitions

- ✳ Green candle
- ✳ Your preferred lighting tool, such as matches or a lighter
- ✳ Paper, pink and/or green preferred
- ✳ Writing tool, pink and/or green preferred

- ✳ Crystals for luck and positivity, such as citrine, crazy lace agate, emerald, malachite, and rose quartz
- ✳ Alfalfa
- ✳ Allspice
- ✳ Bergamot
- ✳ Cinnamon
- ✳ Marigold
- ✳ Sunflower petals or seeds

1. Light the green candle.

2. On the paper, write a thank you note to your home. Express your gratitude for your time there.

3. Now write an affirmation relating to the sale of your home. For example, I might write, "It has been an honor being steward of this dwelling for the last four years. I've enjoyed my time here and am grateful for it, but life is taking me elsewhere and my time here has ended. I am hereby calling forth a buyer for this home—someone who will cherish it as I have. The sale of this home and my transition to the next will be easy and swift. So be it."

4. Speak your written affirmations aloud. Say them to your house as if you're speaking to a friend.

5. Place the written affirmation and thank you note into the spell jar.

6. Add the citrine, crazy lace agate, emerald, malachite, and rose quartz, or the crystals of your choice, to the spell jar.

7. Add the alfalfa, allspice, bergamot, cinnamon, marigold, and sunflower to the jar.

8. Drip a bit of green wax from your candle into the jar.

9. To activate the spell jar, place it in sunlight for a full day.

If possible, keep this spell jar near the entrance to your home so that prospective buyers pass it when they enter. I'd recommend hiding it or building this spell jar in an opaque jar so that no one will be curious about its contents. Alternatively, you can bury this spell jar in the ground near the entrance to your home or even in a potted plant left on your front porch or stoop.

Successful Job Hunting

Job hunting can be a stressful process. This spell jar will help you meet the challenge head-on with confidence and luck on your side. Designed to attract financial prosperity, good fortune, and success in any endeavor you put your mind to, this spell jar will give you the edge you need to land your dream job.

* Green or orange candle
* Your preferred lighting tool, such as matches or a lighter
* Listing for the job you want, or a written description of your ideal job
* Writing tool, gold or green preferred
* Coin currency of any denomination

* Crystals that promote focus, good luck, and success, such as emerald, pyrite, red aragonite, and red zircon
* Alfalfa
* Allspice
* Bergamot
* Blackberry leaf
* Cinnamon
* Gold glitter

1. Light the candle.

2. Read over the job listing. While holding it, close your eyes and imagine yourself in that position. You're happy, successful, and thriving.

3. Write a positive affirmation over the job listing, such as, "I am happy, professionally successful, and thriving."

4. Read your affirmation aloud, then place the job listing in the spell jar.

5. Add the coins to the jar.

6. Place the emerald, pyrite, red aragonite, and red zircon, or the crystals of your choice, into the jar.

7. Add the alfalfa, allspice, bergamot, blackberry leaf, and cinnamon.

8. Sprinkle gold glitter on top.

9. Seal the jar using your preferred method.

10. Activate the spell by placing it in sunlight for a full day.

Hold the spell jar for at least a few moments every morning while imagining your job-hunting goals to soak in its confident, prosperous, successful vibes.

Spell Jars for Personal Well-Being

Achieve Clarity

Do you find yourself faced with a complicated predicament? Are you unsure if you have all the facts you need to proceed? Do you feel as though your emotions or other influences may be preventing you from seeing a situation clearly? This spell jar is designed to lift any energetic blockages that may be holding you back and getting in your way. Peppermint and sound cleansing wake up the senses and move stagnant energy to get any muddying influences out of the picture, leaving you with the clarity you deserve.

* White candle
* Your preferred lighting tool, such as matches or a lighter
* Bell, chimes, or singing bowl
* Sea salt
* Crystals to clear energetic blockages and enhance psychic perception, such as black kyanite, selenite, azurite, and lapis lazuli
* Rosemary
* 1 or 2 drops peppermint oil

1. Light the white candle and take a few moments to get into a meditative, calm state. You can either focus on the flame or close your eyes.

2. Ring the bell or strike the chimes or singing bowl to wake up any stagnant energy in the spell space and remove any energetic blockages.

3. Pour the sea salt into the bottom of the jar.

4. Hold the black kyanite or crystal of choice in your hands and speak aloud, in an affirmative form, your desire for clarity. You could say something like, "Nothing is hidden from me. I am level-headed, sensible, and I have the clarity I need to exercise good judgment."

5. Add the black kyanite, selenite, azurite, and lapis lazuli, or your crystals of choice, to the spell jar.

6. Sprinkle in rosemary.

7. To activate the spell, add a drop or two of peppermint oil to the jar.

8. Seal the spell jar using your preferred method.

Place this spell jar centrally in your living space somewhere you'll pass it often, such as your living room.

Balance Emotions

This spell jar is intended to help restore balance between your head and heart. Every now and again, we all go through times when our emotions are tumultuous. It can be exhausting! This spell jar will stimulate your heart chakra and work to eliminate any blockages there that may be causing you grief. Bear in mind that you have to meet this spell halfway. Make sure you're working on the root of your emotional strife and not just using this spell as a Band-Aid. It's intended to support you in your heart-healing journey, but if there's something or someone in your life that's causing the turmoil, it's your job to root it out and face it. This spell jar has your back!

- ✳ Green candle
- ✳ Your preferred lighting tool, such as matches or a lighter
- ✳ Charm in the shape of a heart
- ✳ Paper, pink or green preferred
- ✳ Writing tool, pink or green preferred
- ✳ Crystals known to promote emotional healing and balance, such as malachite, prehnite, and rose quartz, in the shape of hearts or spheres preferred
- ✳ Green tea leaves
- ✳ Pink rose petals

1. Light the green candle.

2. Place the heart-shaped charm in front of the lit candle to charge.

3. On the paper, write the goal of your spell jar in affirmation form, such as, "My emotions are balanced, and I am at peace. My heart is open, calm, and stable. Energy flows freely through my heart chakra."

4. Speak your written intentions aloud, then roll or fold them up and place the paper in the jar.

5. Add the malachite, prehnite, and rose quartz, or your crystals of choice, to the jar.

6. Add the green tea leaves and pink rose petals to the jar.

7. Seal the spell jar using your preferred method.

8. Activate the spell by gently tapping the jar with your finger or preferred magickal tool while imagining in your mind's eye the goal of your spell jar coming to fruition.

Keep this spell jar in your bedroom. Alternatively, if there's a particular place where your emotions are most in need of balance, such as a work desk if your job is the root of your emotional strife, you can keep the spell jar there.

Become Brave

Everyone feels apprehensive and scared from time to time. When you find yourself unnerved, this spell jar can help to boost your bravery. Imbued with the powerful, compassionate, fearless energy of the Strength tarot card, and with a bit of pyrite for luck, this spell jar will bolster your courage to see you through frightening times.

* Red candle
* Your preferred lighting tool, such as matches or a lighter
* Crystals for fortitude, energy, and luck, such as bloodstone, carnelian, dendritic agate, garnet, and pyrite

* Strength tarot card
* Mullein
* Thyme

1. Light the red candle.

2. Speak aloud an affirmation about bravery. You could say something such as, "I am brave, steadfast, courageous, and coolheaded. My strength will see me to victory."

3. Place the Strength tarot card into the jar.

4. Add the bloodstone, carnelian, dendritic agate, garnet, and pyrite, or your crystals of choice, to the spell jar.

5. Sprinkle the mullein and thyme on top.

6. Activate the spell by gently tapping the jar with your finger or preferred magickal tool while imagining in your mind's eye the goal of your spell jar coming to fruition.

7. Seal this spell jar using your preferred method.

Consider attaching clear quartz to the jar with twine to amplify its energy, or place the jar among lots of clear quartz.

Boost Creativity

Are you feeling stuck in a creative rut? Never fear! This spell jar is designed to remove any energetic blockages that are holding you back from reaching your full creative potential. Craft this spell jar and you'll be brimming with innovative ideas again in no time.

* Orange candle
* Your preferred lighting tool, such as matches or a lighter
* Bay leaf
* Writing tool, red and orange preferred
* Fire-safe receptacle in which you can burn a bay leaf, such as a cast-iron cauldron
* Queen of Wands tarot card
* Crystals that boost focus and creativity, such as red aragonite, red zircon, and vanadinite
* Allspice
* Cinnamon
* Dried orange slice or orange zest

1. Light the orange candle.

2. On the bay leaf, write an affirmation about your creative goals, such as, "Productive, creative energy flows through me freely." If you're concerned that you might not be able to fit an affirmation on your bay leaf with your chosen writing tool, you

can simplify it by writing, "I am creative," or simply the word "creativity."

3. In your fire-safe receptacle, burn the bay leaf.

4. Add the Queen of Wands tarot card to the jar.

5. Place the red aragonite, red zircon, and vanadinite, or your crystals of choice, in the spell jar.

6. Add the allspice, cinnamon, and orange to the jar.

7. Sprinkle the ashes from the incinerated bay leaf on top.

8. Seal the spell jar using your preferred method.

9. To activate the spell, create energetic momentum by gently shaking it.

Keep this spell jar wherever you need a boost of creativity, such as your desk or workspace. Gently shake the jar periodically to cleanse and amplify its magick.

Express Gratitude Spell Jar

It's easy to get bogged down under everyday stress and pressure, and lose sight of all the positivity in your life. Because let's face it: life is filled with challenges, but there are always things to be grateful for, even when you're struggling. It all feels more manageable and positive when we stay in touch with gratitude, which is what this spell jar is designed to help you with.

* Paper, pink preferred
* Writing tool, pink preferred
* Stone from your garden or property, or a menilite opal (also called a fairy stone)
* Crystals that promote gratitude and emotional balance, such as amethyst, chrysocolla, moonstone, and rainbow fluorite
* Herbs that are known to connect you with gratitude by reminding you of all the goodness life has to offer, such as cedar, lavender, and marigold
* Full Moon Water (see page 160 for the Full Moon Water Spell Jar recipe)

1. On your paper, make a list of ten things you're grateful for.

2. Hold your garden or fairy stone in the palm of your hand and read aloud the gratitude list you've made. This will charge the stone with grateful energy.

3. Place the crystals that you've gathered to promote gratitude into the jar.

4. Add your gratitude list to the jar.

5. Add the herbs to the jar.

6. To activate the spell, fill the jar with Full Moon Water until its contents are submerged.

7. Seal the jar using your preferred method. Keep your garden or fairy stone just outside the spell jar.

When you want to recharge the spell jar, hold the garden or fairy stone in your palms and list aloud things you're grateful for.

Find Joy

Are you feeling glum? Down in the dumps? Is life feeling monotonous? Never fear! This spell jar will help to shake you out of the doldrums and reconnect with joy. It's important that elements used in the jar resonate with you personally and bring you joy. For instance, if you absolutely loved LEGOs as a kid, consider using a LEGO in the spell jar to symbolize the joy you've received from them. For best results, customize this spell jar to suit your vision of joyfulness.

* Yellow candle
* Your preferred lighting tool, such as matches or a lighter
* Photo of yourself from a time when you were truly happy
* Sun tarot card

* Crystals with sunny, happy, playful vibes, such as citrine, green jade, pyrite, and sunstone
* Charm or object that symbolizes joy for you personally (see notes)
* Colorful confetti (see notes)

1. Light the yellow candle.

2. Reflect on the photo of yourself from a time when you were truly happy. Recall that feeling of joy and connect with it as you assemble the spell jar.

3. Place The Sun tarot card into the spell jar.

4. Add the citrine, green jade, pyrite, and sunstone, or your crystals of choice.

5. Add the charm or object you connect with joyfulness to the spell jar.

6. Place the photo of yourself in the jar.

7. Sprinkle the colorful confetti into the jar to activate the spell.

8. Seal the jar using your preferred method.

Decorate this spell jar with bright colors, or in ways that bring you joy. Consider using colorful washi tape to seal and decorate the jar, or attach fun beads. Give the jar a gentle shake or swirl to reinvigorate its magick. Surround this spell jar with clear quartz to amplify its energy even more.

Notes:

CHARM: This can be a favorite childhood toy, a ticket stub from an event that made you feel truly elated, or simply a smiley face drawn on paper.

CONFETTI: Choose confetti in colors and shapes that symbolize happiness to you. For example, I use metallic confetti in star, sun, and unicorn shapes. You could also make your own using construction paper.

Honor and Heal Your Inner Child

Many of us have deep wounds from our childhoods that have persisted through the years and affect us to this day. This spell jar supports your inner child and helps you move on from the baggage created by unmet needs or upsetting periods in your childhood.

* Green or pink candle
* Your preferred lighting tool, such as matches or a lighter
* Photo of yourself as a child
* Writing tool that will write well on the photo
* Crystals for protection and emotional healing, such as black tourmaline, blue kyanite, prehnite, rose quartz, and shungite
* Blueberries (see notes)
* Marigold
* Thistle
* 1 or 2 drops vanilla essential oil

1. Light the candle.

2. Hold the photo of yourself as a child. Keep your child-self in mind when creating this jar.

3. With the writing tool, write a comforting statement to your child-self. This can be as long or short as you want it to be. Write on top of the photo, on the back of it, or use additional sheets of paper if you need more space. Tell yourself the things you needed to hear when you were a child that went unsaid.

4. Use wax from the candle to seal your words. If you wrote on the photo, drip the wax over your words. If you needed more space and used additional sheets of paper, fold them up and seal them with wax from the candle.

5. Add the photo and your writings to the spell jar.

6. Place the black tourmaline, blue kyanite, prehnite, rose quartz, and shungite, or your crystals of choice in the jar.

7. Add the blueberries, marigold, and thistle.

8. Activate the spell by adding a drop or two of vanilla essential oil.

9. Seal the jar using your preferred method.

Keep this spell jar somewhere private, away from curious eyes. This is just for you. Consider keeping it in a closet or jewelry box. Periodically recharge the spell by putting rose quartz on or around the spell jar.

Notes: If you'd like to eventually retrieve ingredients from this jar and are concerned about mold, use dried blueberries.

Manifest Good Luck

Whether you've found yourself in a string of unfortunate events and are looking to turn your luck around, or you have an important goal in mind for which you're looking to manifest a lucky boost, this spell jar is designed to attract good fortune into your life. Green and gold are magickally lucky colors, so keep that in mind when choosing charms and objects to include. If the objects are green or gold, their lucky energy is amplified.

* Green candle
* Your preferred lighting tool, such as matches or a lighter
* Charms, beads, and other small objects that represent good luck to you (see notes)
* Basil
* Cinnamon
* Dried orange slices or orange zest
* Crystals for protection and good luck, such as green aventurine, green jade, pyrite, and white jade
* Honey, or another gold liquid, such as champagne, or even metallic paint (see notes)

1. Light the green candle.

2. Place your lucky charms and symbols in front of the candle to charge while you assemble the rest of your spell jar.

3. Add the basil, cinnamon, and orange elements to the jar.

4. Add the green aventurine, green jade, pyrite, and white jade, or your crystals of choice.

5. Gather your lucky charms and hold them in your hands so that both palms are touching them. Close your eyes and visualize yourself as being lucky, happy, and carefree. When you feel ready, add the charms to the spell jar.

6. Drizzle your golden liquid into the spell jar to activate it (or, if you're containing the liquid, place it inside the spell jar).

7. Seal the spell jar using your preferred method.

I recommend decorating this spell jar with good luck symbols and sealing it with a sigil representing good luck. For more on creating sigils, see page 42. Keep this jar near you. On days that I need extra luck, I carry this spell jar with me in my purse. Otherwise, place it somewhere you'll be near it often, such as a work desk, bedside table, or your car, if you have a daily commute.

Notes:

CHARMS: Symbols of good luck could include four-leaf clovers, wishbones, horseshoes, etc. You could also consider using lucky symbols from your religious or cultural background. If you don't have such beads or charms on hand, feel free to draw the chosen symbols on paper or carve them into wooden disks.

HONEY: If you're using ingredients in this spell jar that you'd like to retrieve later and are concerned about the mess, you can contain the golden liquid in a smaller jar, vial, or bag and include it in this spell jar that way.

Spell Jars for the Modern Witch

Manifest Self-Confidence

Have you been feeling insecure lately? Self-critical? We all go through periods of self-doubt and doldrums. If you've lost a bit of your self-confidence, this spell jar will help you hold your head high again and bring back your confident strut. It will remind you of your best qualities and show you what a powerful, strong, capable person you really are.

* Orange candle
* Your preferred lighting tool, such as matches or a lighter
* Paper, pink, red, and/or orange preferred
* Writing tool, pink, red, and/or orange preferred
* Mirror

* Crystals that promote inner strength, power, and fortitude, such as amber, bloodstone, carnelian, garnet, and red jasper
* Ginseng
* Peach pit
* Dried lemon slices, lemon zest, or lemon oil
* Valerian

1. Light the candle.

2. Write powerful self-confidence affirmations on one side of the paper. Make them personal, and tailor them to any issues that may be blocking you from achieving confidence. For example, if the words and opinions of others have negatively affected your self-perception, you could write something like, "I am strong, powerful, and deserving. I don't need everyone to love me because I love and respect myself."

3. Look into the mirror and read your affirmations aloud to your reflection. Repeat them until they really start to resonate with you.

4. On the other side of the paper, list your favorite things about yourself. Are you compassionate? Great at a hobby or skill? What's your favorite physical feature? Write it all down!

5. Read your list aloud to your reflection.

6. Add the amber, bloodstone, carnelian, garnet, and red jasper, or your crystals of choice, to the jar.

7. Add your written affirmation and list to the jar.

8. Add the ginseng, peach pit, lemon ingredient, and valerian to the jar.

9. Seal this spell jar using your preferred method.

10. Activate the spell by placing the jar in sunlight for an hour.

Keep this spell jar somewhere you'll see it every morning, such as at a vanity, on a bathroom counter, or at the beverage station where you prepare your morning coffee or tea.

Promote Your Own Happiness and Well-Being

While I don't believe that witchcraft and other magickal practices can cure diseases or independently heal physical ailments, and I think you should be wary of anyone who promotes such things, I am confident that spellwork can lift your spirits and promote your overall well-being. Healing and health involve the mind, body, and soul. This spell jar is intended to keep your energy centers open to healing and happiness while you work to support your health using conventional means.

Spell Jars for the Modern Witch

- ✳ Yellow candle
- ✳ Your preferred lighting tool, such as matches or a lighter
- ✳ Photo of yourself smiling genuinely from a time when you were happy and feeling your best
- ✳ X of Cups tarot card
- ✳ Crystals that promote health, happiness, and balance, such as amethyst, chrysoprase, green aventurine, and rose quartz
- ✳ Chamomile
- ✳ Echinacea
- ✳ Thistle

1. Light the candle.

2. Hold the photo of yourself and recall how great you were feeling when it was taken. Manifest that feeling and channel it into the spell jar creation process.

3. Add the photo to the spell jar.

4. Add the X of Cups tarot card to the jar.

5. Place the amethyst, chrysoprase, green aventurine, and rose quartz, or your crystals of choice, in the jar.

6. Add the chamomile, echinacea, and thistle.

7. Seal the jar using your preferred method.

8. Activate the spell by placing it in sunlight for at least an hour, but a full day is recommended.

Keep this spell jar in your bedroom or living space. Take care not to place it too near your bed, though, because its effects can be energizing and stimulating, which could interfere with your sleep.

Spell Jars for Work or School

Cultivate a Positive Work Environment

Whether or not a work environment is positive is often a complicated issue. Workers need to be compensated and treated fairly, hours and obligations need to be reasonable, etc. While this spell jar won't be able to magically fix payroll or scheduling issues, it will uplift the vibes around you and protect your workspace so that you're not energetically bogged down by low-vibrational workplace negativity and stress. Keeping your space energetically fresh and unencumbered will attract good luck, positivity, and success. I think we could all use these at work!

* Symbols of your job or workplace (see notes)
* Crystals for positivity and dispelling negativity, such as black kyanite, opal, selenite, and sunstone
* Allspice
* Chamomile
* Marigold
* Nettle leaf
* Peppermint
* Full Moon Water (see page 160 for the Full Moon Water Spell Jar recipe)
* Blue glitter and/or metallic confetti

1. Add the symbols of your job or workplace to the spell jar.

2. Place the black kyanite, opal, selenite, and sunstone, or your crystals of choice, in the spell jar.

3. Add the allspice, chamomile, marigold, nettle leaf, and peppermint.

4. Fill the spell jar with Full Moon Water until everything is submerged.

5. Sprinkle some blue glitter or confetti on top.

6. Seal the spell jar using your preferred method.

7. To activate the spell, create energetic momentum by gently shaking it.

Keep this jar at your workspace, such as in a desk drawer or on your work desk. To refresh the spell jar and get a boost of its magick, give the spell jar a swirl or gentle shake.

Notes: I was a dog groomer for several years, so if I were creating this spell jar to promote positivity during that career, I might add a charm in the shape of a cat or dog, miniature scissors to represent my grooming shears, or a bit of dog hair (because you get covered in it every day as a groomer!).

Encourage a Cohesive Collaboration

We all know that working with other people isn't always as seamless and problem-free as it can be. Everyone has different perspectives, ideas, and communication styles, and while that diversity is what makes collaborations so great, it can also lead to miscommunications and disagreements. Create this spell jar to encourage cohesive, productive, smooth collaboration anytime you need to get together with others to accomplish a goal.

Spell Jars for Work or School

- ✳ Paper, blue preferred
- ✳ Writing tool, blue preferred
- ✳ III of Cups tarot card (see notes)
- ✳ Crystals that open up the throat chakra to promote easy communication, such as blue apatite, chrysocolla, sodalite, and turquoise
- ✳ Full Moon Water (see page 160 for the Full Moon Water Spell Jar recipe)

1. On the paper, write affirmations relating to your collaboration and its goal. For example, if I were working on a collaboration to launch a startup company, I might write, "The team and I respect each other's talents and the unique perspectives we each bring to this company. Our communication is easy and smooth, which allows us to contribute our best efforts to make this startup successful."

2. Speak the written affirmations aloud.

3. Add the written affirmations to the spell jar.

4. Add the III of Cups tarot card to the jar.

5. Add the blue apatite, chrysocolla, sodalite, and turquoise, or your crystals of choice, to the jar.

6. To activate the spell, add Full Moon Water to the jar until all the contents are submerged.

7. Seal the spell jar using your preferred method.

Keep this spell jar in your workspace, such as on a shelf in your office, or, if you're a student and this is a collaboration for school, in your backpack. Have it near you whenever you're working on your collaborative goal. Place it in sunlight whenever you'd like to charge it, to wake up any stagnant energy and refresh the spell with positive, happy vibes.

> **Notes:** The III of Cups tarot card represents collaboration and community. Know that this tarot card will be submerged in water, so consider using a card from a plastic tarot deck, or a tarot card from a deck you don't mind sacrificing for spellwork. An acrylic or metal jewelry pendant featuring the III of Cups tarot card is acceptable, too.

Financial Abundance

I think it's safe to say that financial abundance and material comfort are major goals for most of us. Who among us doesn't want a comfortable life without financial worry and strife? Whether you are looking to manifest a lucrative new job or opportunity, about to ask your boss for the raise you deserve, or looking for lucky vibes as you buy lottery tickets, this spell jar is created to radiate lucky energy and attract financial and material abundance.

* Green or gold candle
* Your preferred lighting tool, such as matches or a lighter
* Paper, green and/or gold preferred
* Writing tool, green and/or gold preferred
* X of Pentacles tarot card (see notes)
* Coins or cash of any denomination
* Objects you associate with good luck, such as four-leaf clovers or horseshoe charms (see notes)
* Alfalfa
* Ash
* Bergamot
* Cinnamon
* Green and gold glitter or confetti

1. Light the candle.

2. On the paper, write affirmations relating to financial abundance. If you have a specific financial goal in mind, include that. For example, if I were trying to get a promotion and raise at work, I might write, "My hard work is recognized and financially rewarded. I am achieving, and deserving of, financial abundance."

3. Speak the written affirmations aloud.

4. Fold the written affirmations and seal them with wax from the candle. Then place the written affirmations into the spell jar.

5. Add the X of Pentacles tarot card to the jar.

6. Add the coins or cash to the jar.

7. Add the objects associated with good luck.

8. Add the green jade, pyrite, and tiger's eye, or your crystals of choice, to the spell jar.

9. Add the alfalfa, ash, bergamot, and cinnamon.

10. Add the green and gold glitter or confetti.

11. Seal the spell jar using your preferred method.

12. To activate the spell, create energetic momentum by gently shaking it.

Charge this spell jar in sunlight and give it a gentle shake or swirl whenever you need a boost of its lucky, successful magick.

Notes:

TAROT CARD: The X of Pentacles tarot card represents financial abundance and material comforts.

OBJECTS: If you have any personally lucky items, such as a lucky penny or stone, include those, too. Green is a lucky color, so the lucky vibes are enhanced if objects you choose to include are green.

Manifest Motivation

Has life become a bit monotonous? Have you lost touch with the passion and drive necessary to achieve your goals? Perhaps you've lost sight of your goals altogether. That's okay! We all feel stuck in slumps every now and again. This spell jar is designed to reinvigorate stagnant energy and reconnect you with your sense of drive and motivation. This spell jar honors and includes the elements Air and Fire, which will work together to lift you out of stagnancy and inspire you.

* Orange candle
* Your preferred lighting tool, such as matches or a lighter
* Bell or chimes
* The Chariot tarot card, which represents movement and drive
* Crystals to promote energy and optimism, such as carnelian, mookaite jasper, red aragonite, and red zircon
* Cinnamon
* Nettle leaf
* Dried orange peels or slices
* Passionflower
* Yarrow
* 1 drop citrus essential oil

1. Light the candle.

2. Ring the bell or play the chimes to clear out any stagnant energy and prime your space for magick.

3. Add The Chariot tarot card to the spell jar.

4. Add the carnelian, mookaite jasper, red aragonite, and red zircon, or your crystals of choice, to the jar.

5. Add the cinnamon, nettle leaf, dried orange, passionflower, and yarrow.

6. To activate the spell, place a drop of the energizing citrus essential oil under the lid of the jar before sealing.

Charge this spell jar in sunlight for a full twelve-hour day. Keep it at your workspace, or wherever you need motivation the most. Hold it with both palms whenever you need a boost of energy and inspiration.

Spell Jars for Animals or Children

Promote the Well-Being of a Child

This spell jar is intended to support a child's wellness, happiness, and growth. You can create it for your own children, or the children of a loved one, such as nieces, nephews, or cousins . If the subject of the spell jar isn't your own child, I suggest getting permission from the parents before performing spellwork on their child's behalf, but it's ultimately up to you to reflect on your own ethics about this.

* Sea salt
* Item representing the child (see notes)
* Paper, green or pink preferred
* Writing tool, green or pink preferred
* Crystals promoting wellness and longevity, such as garnet, green aventurine, and nephrite jade
* Crystals known to connect with the joyful, compassionate, innocent nature of children, such as dalmatian, jasper, and rose quartz
* Acorn
* Blueberries
* Thistle
* 1 or 2 drops eucalyptus essential oil
* Clear quartz points, at least three

1. Pour the sea salt into the jar to create a base layer on which to rest the other ingredients.

2. Add the item you choose to represent the child.

3. On the paper, write an affirmation encapsulating the goal of this spell jar. For example, "[Child's name] is thriving, happy, and divinely protected from negative influences."

4. Add the written affirmation to the spell jar.

5. Add all of the crystals to the jar.

6. Place the acorn, blueberries, and thistle on top.

7. To activate the spell, add a drop or two of eucalyptus essential oil to the jar before sealing it using your preferred method.

Ideally, this spell jar would be kept safely in the child's room. But if you've created this for a loved one who doesn't live in the home with you, place this jar in the spot of your home that's nearest their home. For example, if the child lives several miles northwest of you, place the jar in the northwest corner of your home. Then, place clear quartz points outside the jar pointing in that same direction to direct the spell's energy and magick toward the child's home.

Notes: An item representing the child could be a photo, ideally taken of the child during a time of happiness and good health, an object belonging to the child, or a trinket or charm that symbolizes them in some way.

Promote the Well-Being of an Animal

Many of us have animals in our lives that we love very much. This spell jar can be created for your pets, loved ones' pets, stray animals, or shelter animals whose welfare you're concerned about, etc. I used this recipe for a stray dog that I'd been working with a local animal rescue to try to catch for weeks. She was scared, skittish, and difficult to catch. I wanted to send positive, healing energy her way, so I made this spell jar using a photograph of her. Thankfully, she was finally caught safe and sound about a week later.

※ Brown candle

※ Your preferred lighting tool, such as matches or a lighter

※ Items representing the animal (see notes)

※ Drawing or photograph of the animal

※ Crystals for grounding, longevity, and stability, such as amber, garnet, obsidian, and red jasper

※ Catnip

※ Chickweed

※ Juniper berries

1. Light the candle.

2. Add the gathered items representing the animal to the spell jar.

3. Hold the drawing or photograph of the animal in both hands. Close your eyes, and imagine the animal healthy, happy, and thriving. While that image is still fresh in your mind's eye, carefully drip a bit of candle wax from the brown candle onto the photo or drawing to seal in that positive energy.

4. Add the photograph or drawing to the spell jar.

Spell Jars for Animals or Children

5. Add the amber, garnet, obsidian, and red jasper, or your crystals of choice, to the jar.

6. Add the catnip, chickweed, and juniper berries.

7. Seal the spell jar using your preferred method.

8. Activate the spell by gently tapping the jar with your finger or preferred magickal tool while envisioning the subject of the spell thriving, happy, and healthy.

Ideally, this spell jar would be kept near the pet (but safely out of its reach!), such as on a shelf near their bed or a counter by their feeding station.

> **Notes:** Ethically collected biological material from the animal is preferred, such as feathers, fur, or saved baby teeth or teeth from dental extractions. You could also include items closely connected with the animal, such as a bit of water from its tank in the case of aquatic animals, an old identification tag that was worn by the animal, or a favorite toy or treats. Beads or charms in the shape of the animal this spell jar is for will work as well.

Spell Jars for the Modern Witch

Protect an Animal or Pet

This spell jar is intended to manifest and direct protective magick and energy to an animal or pet. Unfortunately, in the real world, there's no way to use magick in a way that physically protects in a 100 percent foolproof way. I wish I could conjure a patronus Harry Potterstyle and send it to fiercely protect and defend loved ones, but that's just not how things work. This spell jar, when used with real-world common sense and protective action, is the next-best thing.

* Black candle
* Your preferred lighting tool, such as matches or a lighter
* Item representing the animal (see notes)
* Cotton balls
* Rose quartz
* Crystals for good luck and protection, such as black tourmaline, garnet, green jade, and hematite

* 1 bay leaf
* Catnip
* Clove
* Pine needles
* Sharp objects, such as push pins, open safety pins, or sewing needles
* Sprinkle of black pepper
* Full Moon Water (see page 160 for the Full Moon Water Spell Jar recipe)

1. Light the black candle.

2. Hold the item representing the animal, and envision the animal being enveloped in a protective sphere of bright light.

3. Add a layer of cotton balls to the bottom of the jar, then place the item and the rose quartz on top. Add another layer of cotton over them, symbolizing a loving, protective buffer keeping the animal from harm.

4. Add the crystals for good luck and protection.

5. Add the bay leaf, catnip, clove, and pine needles.

6. Add the sharp objects, symbolizing protective, defensive energy.

7. Sprinkle black pepper into the jar for protection.

8. Say a protective affirmation aloud. For example, "My canine companion, Rumpel, is loved, safe, and supernaturally protected from harm."

9. To activate the spell, add Full Moon Water to the jar. Ideally, you would add enough so that the jar's contents are submerged, but any amount of Full Moon Water will work in a pinch.

10. Seal the spell jar using your preferred method.

I recommend encasing protective spell jars in black wax. Charge the spell jar overnight in moonlight and keep it somewhere where it will be safe from curious eyes or hands. When it needs a charge, place it in moonlight again.

Notes: Ethically collected biological material from the animal is preferred, such as feathers, fur, or saved baby teeth or teeth from dental extractions. Alternatively, you could use an old identification tag that was worn by the animal, or a bead or charm in the shape of the animal.

Spell Jars for the Modern Witch

Spell Jars for Protection

Banish Bad Vibes

Have you found yourself in an energetically heavy situation? Do you feel bombarded by bad news and negativity? Release yourself from the grip of low-vibrational energy using this spell jar. Consider creating a miniature version of it in a wearable vial using crystal chips and small amounts of the listed herbs. It's a great spell jar to carry with you all day long.

* Black candle
* Your preferred lighting tool, such as matches or a lighter
* Paper, black preferred
* Writing tool, black preferred
* Crystals for protection and banishing negativity, such as black kyanite, black obsidian, black tourmaline, and labradorite
* Black pepper
* Peppermint
* Pine needles
* Multiple clear quartz points or tumbles

1. Light the candle.

2. On the paper, write an affirmation relating to the goal of the spell jar, such as, "My aura repels negative energy. My spiritual boundaries are firm, and I am protected by negative influence."

3. Speak the written affirmation aloud. If you feel you need to repeat it, do so until you truly believe your words and feel the power in them.

4. Add the written affirmation to the spell jar.

5. Add the protective crystals to the jar.

6. Add the black pepper, peppermint, and pine needles.

7. After sealing the spell jar, activate the spell by surrounding it with clear quartz to amplify its magick in all directions.

Place the spell jar where you feel energetically weighed-down the most. For example, if you're feeling a lot of negative energy at work, place the spell jar on your desk or in a desk drawer. If media, such as the news, is making you feel heavy-hearted, consider placing this spell jar near your television set, radio, cell phone while it's charging, or wherever else you get your news.

Promote Safe Travel

Travel can certainly be nerve-wracking and anxiety-inducing. Take this spell jar with you on your journeys, whether long or short, to promote easy and safe travel. Personally, I created this spell jar and keep it in the glove box of my husband's vehicle to help protect him during his long commutes to and from work.

✳ III of Wands tarot card

✳ Items symbolizing travel, such as beads or charms in the shape of cars, planes, or boats, or photos or drawings of the like

* Items symbolizing good luck, such as beads or charms in the shape of four-leaf clovers, horseshoes, or any items that you personally associate with good luck (see notes)

* Crystals for good luck, grounding, and protection during travel, such as bloodstone, labradorite, and shungite.

* Acorn

* Mullein

* Sunflower petals or seeds

1. Place the III of Wands tarot card into your spell jar.

2. Add the items symbolizing travel.

3. Hold the spell jar in your hands and visualize your journey and destination. Imagine arriving at your destination feeling energized, happy, and healthy.

4. Add the items symbolizing good luck to the spell jar.

5. Add the crystals to the spell jar.

6. Place the acorn, mullein, and sunflower on top.

7. Activate the spell by gently tapping the jar with your finger or preferred magickal tool while imagining yourself traveling safely and comfortably.

8. Seal the spell jar using your preferred method, but make sure to avoid using wax if it will be kept in a place that gets warm, such as a car or in luggage, as wax can melt and make a big mess.

Take the spell jar with you during travel. You can pack it in luggage or keep it in your vehicle.

Notes: Gold and green are lucky colors, so you can include items of those colors to symbolize good luck if you'd like.

Protection from Nightmares

Are you plagued by nightmares? Longing for a restful, undisturbed sleep? This spell jar will help you banish boogeymen and bad vibes so you can once again enjoy the peaceful sleep you need to feel your very best.

* Black candle
* Your preferred lighting tool, such as matches or a lighter
* Paper, purple or black preferred
* Writing tool, purple or black preferred
* Sea salt
* Chamomile
* Lavender
* Protective crystals, such as black tourmaline, black obsidian, and/or black kyanite
* Clear quartz sphere

1. Light the black candle.

2. On the paper, write a protective affirmation, such as, "I am protected, undisturbed, and peaceful as I sleep."

3. Pour in the sea salt to create a protective base for the spell.

4. Add the chamomile and lavender to the jar.

5. Add the protective crystals to the jar.

6. To activate the spell, add the clear quartz sphere. This radiates the energy of the spell evenly throughout your space.

7. Seal the jar using your preferred method.

Consider decorating this spell jar with dried lavender or chamomile to amplify its magickal effects. Place the spell jar under or beside your bed; just make sure it's near you while you sleep to get the most benefit from its protective power.

Protect Your Living Space

Living spaces need regular cleansing—not just physically, but energetically, too! We carry our stresses and worries home with us at the end of the day, and it's important to clear out those heavy vibes so we can move through our homes unencumbered by old, stagnant energy. This spell jar is designed to do just that! It will also protect your living space by turning away any negative energy or entities that may try to darken your doorstep, so your home stays a peaceful, happy haven.

* Black candle
* Your preferred lighting tool, such as matches or a lighter
* Clear quartz, preferably in a cube, pyramid, or sphere shape
* Bell or chime
* Paper, black preferred
* Writing tool, black preferred

* (Optional) Objects that represent protection to you personally (see notes)
* Crystals for protection, such as black tourmaline, black onyx, and labradorite
* Angelica
* Basil
* Coriander
* Peppermint
* Pumpkin seeds

Spell Jars for Protection

1. Light the candle and place the clear quartz in front of it to radiate the spell's magick throughout the space.

2. Ring the bell or play the chimes to awaken any stagnant energy and call attention to your spell.

3. On the paper, write an affirmation related to the goal of the spell jar, such as, "My home is fiercely protected from negative energy and forces. Only those with good intentions are welcome here."

4. Speak the affirmation aloud and add it to the spell jar.

5. Add any gathered objects that represent protection to the spell jar.

6. Add the protective crystals.

7. Add the angelica, basil, coriander, peppermint, and pumpkin seeds to the spell jar.

8. Activate the spell by gently tapping the jar with your finger or preferred magickal tool while envisioning your living space bathed in brilliant, bright, protective light.

9. Seal the jar using your preferred method.

Keep this spell jar in a central location in your home, or near the main entrance. You can also bury the spell jar in your yard to radiate its protective energy throughout your land, which is what I've personally done. I've made two of these spell jars; one is buried in my front yard and the other in the backyard.

Notes: Objects of protection differs for each person. For example, some cultures view dragons as protective, so people of that culture would include an object in the shape of a dragon or that features an image of a dragon. Personally, I work with elementals in magick and feel that gnomes are protective earth spirits, so I include a little gnome figurine in this spell jar. If there's a certain animal, object, or figure that symbolizes protection and resonates with you personally, feel free to include a representation of it.

Protect Your Peace
(A Spell Jar for Empaths)

This is a great spell jar for empaths, or others who are easily influenced emotionally or energetically by the moods and vibes of those around them. It's intended to form an energetic boundary, preventing you from being drained or overly influenced by outside forces.

* Black candle
* Your preferred lighting tool, such as matches or a lighter
* Paper, black preferred
* Writing tool, black preferred
* Crystals known for balancing emotions and grounding, such as malachite, smoky quartz, and shungite

* Juniper
* Mullein
* Rosemary
* Willow
* Yarrow
* 1 or 2 drops pine essential oil

1. Light the candle.

2. On the paper, write an affirmation relating to the goal of the spell, such as, "A powerful, magickal boundary protects me from being drained by the emotions and energetic vibrations of those around me. I am grounded and protected."

3. Speak aloud your written affirmation. Repeat it as necessary until it completely resonates with you.

4. Fold your written affirmation and seal the folded paper shut with wax from the black candle. Add it to the spell jar.

5. Add the gathered crystals to the spell jar.

6. Add the juniper, mullein, rosemary, willow, and yarrow to the jar.

7. Place a drop or two of pine essential oil over the contents of the jar to activate the spell.

8. Seal the jar using your preferred method.

Consider making this spell jar in a small vial that you can wear as jewelry to carry its protection with you wherever you go. Alternatively, you can carry it with you in a bag, pocket, or purse.

Spell Jars for the Modern Witch

Cosmic Spell Jars

Astrological Season Spell Jars

This dynamic collection of astrological season spell jars has been created to help you make the most out of the unique energetic advantages and features of each season. You can make them for your sign (I recommend going by either your natal Moon or Sun sign) and keep them around all year to honor your sign and take the most advantage of its special qualities. I've also found that these make great gifts!

Aries Season

Aries is a confident, driven, expressive sign that's always up for a challenge. Create this spell jar to honor Aries season and harness the fiery qualities of The Ram.

* Orange or red candle
* Your preferred lighting tool, such as matches or a lighter
* Paper, red preferred
* Writing tool, red preferred
* Diamond and clear quartz (see notes)
* The Emperor tarot card
* Bergamot
* Honeysuckle
* 1 or 2 drops peppermint essential oil

1. Light the candle.

2. On the paper, write an affirmation relating to the intrinsic qualities of Aries that you're looking to magnify and embrace for yourself or an Aries friend, such as, "I am ambitious, courageous, and self-expressive."

3. Say the written affirmation aloud. Repeat until it truly resonates with you.

4. Fold the written affirmation, seal it with wax from the candle, and add it to the spell jar.

5. Add the diamond and clear quartz to the spell jar.

6. Add The Emperor tarot card to the jar.

7. Sprinkle in the bergamot and honeysuckle.

8. To activate the spell, add a drop or two of peppermint essential oil.

9. Seal the spell jar using your preferred method.

Be careful not to keep this spell jar close to your bed at night, as its powerful, invigorating energy may interfere with sleep.

Notes: Diamond jewelry is okay to use; it doesn't have to be a loose stone. If a diamond isn't accessible for you, a symbolic diamond can be used, such as cubic zirconia or a glass diamond-like jewel.

Spell Jars for the Modern Witch

Taurus Season

Taurus is the sign of the hard working homebody. Create this spell jar to honor Taurus season and embrace the sensible, steadfast qualities of The Bull.

* Paper, brown or green preferred
* Writing tool, brown or green preferred
* Dirt from your garden or another peaceful, lovely place
* The Hierophant tarot card (see notes)

* Emerald
* Clear quartz
* Sapphire
* Moss
* Poppies
* Violet

1. Begin the spell jar creation process by grounding yourself. Sit with your feet flat on the floor and take a moment to close your eyes, take deep breaths to relax yourself, and bring your focus to the present time.

2. On the paper, write an affirmation relating to the intrinsic qualities of Taurus that you're looking to magnify and embrace for yourself, such as, "I am practical and sensible. These qualities are balanced with the fact that I respect myself enough to value and prioritize my own happiness and self-care."

3. Say the written affirmation aloud. Repeat until it truly resonates with you.

4. Place the dirt in the spell jar.

5. Bury your written affirmations in the spell jar's dirt.

6. Add The Hierophant tarot card to the spell jar.

7. Add the emerald, clear quartz, and sapphire to the jar.

8. Add the moss, poppies, and violet.

9. Seal the spell jar using your preferred method.

10. Activate the spell by burying this spell jar in the ground or a potted plant for 24 hours.

Whenever your emotions feel a bit chaotic or your mind is hectic and lacking focus, use this spell jar for a boost of grounding, stabilizing energy by holding the jar in both hands. Make sure both of your palms touch the jar.

Notes: This will be buried in dirt, so a printed photo or drawn representation of The Hierophant tarot card will do if you don't want to dirty a professionally created tarot card for this spell jar.

Gemini Season

Gemini is an attractive, dynamic, social butterfly who knows a little about a lot of different topics. Create this spell jar to honor Gemini season and embrace the magnetic qualities of The Twins.

* **Bell or chimes**
* **Paper, yellow or bright blue preferred**
* **Writing tool, yellow or bright blue preferred**
* **The Lovers tarot card**
* **Agate**
* **Tiger's eye**
* **Clear quartz**
* **Chrysanthemum**
* **Poplar**
* **1 or 2 drops lavender essential oil**

1. Begin by ringing the bell or playing the chimes to reinvigorate any stagnant energy in your creation space and to honor the element Air, which rules the sign of Gemini.

2. On the paper, write an affirmation relating to the intrinsic qualities of Gemini that you're looking to magnify and embrace for yourself, such as, "I am creative, social, and a unique visionary. I attract connections and friends easily."

3. Say the written affirmation aloud. Repeat until it truly resonates with you.

4. Add the written affirmation to the spell jar.

5. Add The Lovers tarot card to the spell jar.

6. Add the agate, tiger's eye, and clear quartz to the jar.

7. Place the chrysanthemum and poplar on top.

8. To activate the spell, add a drop or two of lavender essential oil.

9. Seal the jar using your preferred method.

Leave this spell jar outside in the wind whenever it needs a recharge. You can also leave it near an open window to catch a stray breeze. If wind isn't forecasted anytime soon, ring a bell or play chimes near the spell jar to charge it.

Cancer Season

The sign of Cancer is emotional, nurturing, and supportive. Create this spell jar to honor Cancer season and embrace the soft, tender, protective magick of The Crab.

* Paper, silver or light blue preferred
* Writing tool, silver or light blue preferred
* The Chariot tarot card (see notes)
* Clear quartz
* Pearl (see notes)
* Moonstone
* Charm, bead, drawing, or other item depicting a mermaid
* Full Moon Water (see page 160 for the Full Moon Water Spell Jar recipe)
* Chickweed
* Magnolia
* White rose petals

1. On the paper, write an affirmation relating to the intrinsic qualities of Cancer that you're looking to magnify and embrace for yourself, such as, "I am compassionate, kind, and intuitive. My friendships and other personal connections are easy, inspiring, and supportive."

2. Say the written affirmation aloud. Repeat until it truly resonates with you.

3. Add the written affirmation to the spell jar.

4. Add The Chariot tarot card to the spell jar.

5. Add the clear quartz, pearl, and moonstone to the jar.

6. Add the mermaid item to the spell jar.

7. To activate the spell, add enough moon water to completely submerge the jar's contents.

8. Place the chickweed, magnolia, and white rose petals on top.

9. Seal the jar using your preferred method.

Whenever this spell jar needs to recharge, place it in moonlight overnight.

Notes:

TAROT CARD: Know that this will be submerged in water, so a printed photo or drawn representation of The Chariot will do if you don't want to sacrifice a professionally created tarot card for this spell jar.

PEARL: If a real pearl isn't accessible or you'd rather not use one, a symbolic pearl can be substituted, such as one made from glass.

Leo Season

Leo is a bold, fearless, loud sign that does everything with an expressive flourish. Create this spell jar to honor Leo season and embrace the inspirational, visionary drama of The Lion.

- ✳ Candle, orange or red preferred
- ✳ Your preferred lighting tool, such as matches or a lighter
- ✳ Paper, gold, orange, or red preferred
- ✳ Writing tool, gold, orange, or red preferred

- ✳ Clear quartz
- ✳ Onyx
- ✳ Ruby
- ✳ Strength tarot card
- ✳ Allspice
- ✳ Marigold
- ✳ Sunflower petals or seeds

1. Light the candle.

2. On the paper, write an affirmation relating to the intrinsic qualities of Leo that you're looking to magnify and embrace for yourself, such as, "I am brave, magnetic, and self-expressive. Others are attracted to my confidence and bold individuality."

3. Say the written affirmation aloud. Repeat until it truly resonates with you.

4. Fold the written affirmation and seal with candle wax. Then place the written affirmation in the spell jar.

5. Add the clear quartz, onyx, and ruby to the spell jar.

6. Add the Strength tarot card to the jar.

7. Add the allspice, marigold, and sunflower to the jar.

8. Seal the jar using your preferred method.

9. To activate the spell, place the jar in sunlight for a full day.

Be careful not to keep it close to your bed at night, as its invigorating energy may interfere with sleep.

Virgo Season

Resourceful Virgos don't get ready; they stay ready. Create this spell jar to honor Virgo season and embrace the meticulous organization and cool sensibility of The Maiden.

✴ **Paper, dark brown or navy blue preferred**

✴ **Writing tool, dark brown or navy blue preferred**

✴ **Dirt from your garden or another lovely, peaceful place**

✴ **The Hermit tarot card (see notes)**

* Carnelian
* Clear quartz
* Sardonyx
* Buttercup

* Cumin
* 1 to 2 drops eucalyptus essential oil

1. On the paper, write an affirmation relating to the intrinsic qualities of Virgo that you're looking to magnify and embrace for yourself, such as, "I am discerning and perceptive. I notice details that others overlook, which helps to inform me with the knowledge and truths I need to make the best possible decisions."

2. Say the written affirmation aloud. Repeat until it truly resonates with you.

3. Add the gathered dirt to the spell jar.

4. Bury your written affirmations in the dirt.

5. Add The Hermit tarot card to the jar.

6. Add the carnelian, clear quartz, and sardonyx.

7. Add the buttercup and cumin.

8. To activate the spell, add a drop or two of eucalyptus essential oil.

9. Seal the jar using a method of your choice.

To make the most of this spell jar's qualities, I recommend keeping this spell jar by your work desk, or another area that tends to get a little messy or chaotic. The spell's effects will help you keep it organized and under control.

Notes: Know that this will be buried in dirt, so a printed photo or drawn representation of The Hermit tarot card will do if you don't want to dirty a professionally created tarot card for this spell jar.

Libra Season

Libra is a social sign that places great value on friendship, love, and beauty. Create this spell jar to honor Libra season and embrace the peace-making social grace of The Scales.

❋ Bell or chimes
❋ Paper, pastel pink preferred
❋ Writing tool, pastel pink preferred
❋ Justice tarot card
❋ Clear quartz
❋ Chrysoprase
❋ Flower agate
❋ Angelica
❋ Daisy
❋ Pink rose petals

1. Ring the bell or play the chimes to reinvigorate any stagnant energy in your creation space and honor the element Air, by which Libra is ruled.

2. On the paper, write an affirmation relating to the intrinsic qualities of Libra that you're looking to magnify and embrace for yourself, such as, "I cultivate beauty all around me. This empowers and inspires me to be the best version of myself. My personal connections and friendships are nurturing, peaceful, and supportive."

3. Say the written affirmation aloud. Repeat until it truly resonates with you.

4. Add the written affirmations to the spell jar.

5. Add the Justice tarot card to the spell jar.

6. Add the clear quartz, chrysoprase, and flower agate to the jar.

7. Add the angelica, daisy, and pink rose petals.

8. Seal the spell jar using your preferred method.

9. To activate the spell, leave the spell jar outside in the wind or near an open window to catch a breeze.

If wind isn't forecasted anytime soon, you can ring a bell or play chimes near the finished spell jar to activate or recharge this spell jar.

Scorpio Season

Calculating Scorpio talks a strong game but bonds deeply and emotionally when they choose to let people into their world. Create this spell jar to honor Scorpio season and embrace the decidedly cool energy of The Scorpion.

* **Paper, black or dark red preferred**
* **Writing tool, black or dark red preferred**
* **Death tarot card (see notes)**
* **Citrine**
* **Clear quartz**
* **Opal**
* **Cardamom**
* **Gardenia**
* **Geranium**
* **Full Moon Water (see page 160 for the Full Moon Water Spell Jar recipe)**

1. On the paper, write an affirmation relating to the intrinsic qualities of Scorpio that you're looking to magnify and

embrace for yourself, such as, "I am cautious and calculating, which helps me make the best possible decisions. My intensity and passion drive me to pursue my goals boldly and make my own dreams come true."

2. Say the written affirmation aloud. Repeat until it truly resonates with you.

3. Add the written affirmations to the spell jar.

4. Add the Death tarot card to the spell jar.

5. Add the crystals.

6. Add the cardamom, gardenia, and geranium.

7. To activate the spell, add enough Moon Water to the jar to fully submerge the ingredients.

8. Seal the jar using your preferred method.

Charge this spell jar in the moonlight whenever it needs a boost of magickal energy and invigoration.

Notes: Know that this will be submerged in water, so a printed photo or drawn representation of the Death tarot card will do if you don't want to sacrifice a professionally created tarot card for this spell jar.

Sagittarius Season

Sagittarius is an idealistic, deep-thinking free spirit who's always up for a new adventure, whether that means jet setting or exploring new worlds and ideas in books. Create this spell jar to honor Sagittarius season and embrace the expansive, lighthearted, lucky energy of The Archer.

- ✳ Candle, dark purple preferred
- ✳ Your preferred lighting tool, such as matches or a lighter
- ✳ Paper, dark purple preferred
- ✳ Writing tool, dark purple preferred
- ✳ Temperance tarot card
- ✳ Clear quartz
- ✳ Topaz
- ✳ Turquoise
- ✳ Carnation
- ✳ Cinnamon
- ✳ Dandelion

1. Light the candle.

2. On the paper, write an affirmation relating to the intrinsic qualities of Sagittarius that you're looking to magnify and embrace for yourself, such as, "I am a dynamic free spirit who trusts that things will always work out in the end. My authenticity and optimism attract good luck and bring all the right people into my life at the right times."

3. Say the written affirmation aloud. Repeat until it truly resonates with you.

4. Fold the written affirmations and seal them with candle wax. Then place the written affirmations into the spell jar.

5. Add the Temperance tarot card to the spell jar.

6. Add the clear quartz, topaz, and turquoise.

7. Add the carnation, cinnamon, and dandelion.

8. Seal the jar using your preferred method.

9. Activate this spell jar by placing it in sunlight for a full day.

Be careful not to keep this spell jar close to your bed at night, as its invigorating energy may interfere with sleep.

Capricorn Season

Ambitious, confident, and cool under pressure, Capricorn is an impressive go-getter who masters their own fate. Create this spell jar to honor Capricorn season and embrace the tenacious, successful power of The Sea-Goat.

* Paper, dark gray or navy preferred
* Writing tool, dark gray or navy preferred
* Dirt from your garden or another lovely, peaceful place

* The Devil tarot card (see notes)
* Clear quartz
* Garnet
* Ivy
* Pansy
* 1 or 2 drops almond essential oil

1. On the paper, write an affirmation relating to the intrinsic qualities of Capricorn that you're looking to magnify and embrace for yourself, such as, "I am ambitious, grounded, and capable of driving my own destiny. I have the knowledge and know-how to make my wildest dreams come true."

2. Say the written affirmations aloud. Repeat until it truly resonates with you.

3. Add the dirt to the spell jar, then bury your written affirmations in the dirt.

4. Add The Devil tarot card to the spell jar, making sure it's upside-down in orientation. When upside-down, The Devil represents freedom, self-sufficiency, and being comfortably in control.

5. Add the clear quartz and garnet to the jar.

6. Place the ivy and pansy on top.

7. To activate the spell, add a drop or two of almond essential oil.

8. Seal the jar using your preferred method.

To recharge this spell jar with grounding energy, bury it in the ground or a potted plant for 24 hours.

Notes: Know that this will be buried in dirt, so a printed photo or drawn representation of the Devil tarot card will do if you don't want to dirty a professionally created tarot card for this spell jar.

Aquarius Season

Aquarius is an innovative, progressive sign with a strong idealistic streak and an eye on the future. Create this spell jar to honor Aquarius season and embrace the potential of a better, brighter future with The Water Bearer.

- ✳ **Bell or chimes**
- ✳ **Paper, teal preferred**
- ✳ **Writing tool, teal preferred**
- ✳ **The Star tarot card**
- ✳ **Amethyst**

- ✳ **Clear quartz**
- ✳ **Cottonwood**
- ✳ **Goldenrod**
- ✳ **Orchid**

1. Ring the bell or play the chimes to reinvigorate any stagnant energy in your creation space and honor the element Air, by which Aquarius is ruled.

2. On the paper, write an affirmation relating to the intrinsic qualities of Aquarius that you're looking to magnify and embrace for yourself, such as, "Embracing nonconformity helps me to create and stay dedicated to my progressive, unique vision for the future. My commitment to this vision inspires others to embrace it and take action to make it a reality."

3. Say the written affirmation aloud. Repeat until it truly resonates with you.

4. Add the written affirmations to the spell jar.

5. Add The Star tarot card to the spell jar.

6. Add the amethyst and clear quartz.

7. Add the cottonwood, goldenrod, and orchid to the spell jar.

8. Seal the jar using your preferred method.

9. To activate the spell, leave the spell jar outside in the wind to charge. Alternatively, leave it near an open window to catch a breeze.

If wind isn't forecasted anytime soon, you can ring a bell or play chimes near the spell jar to activate or recharge it.

Pisces Season

Pisces is an empathetic, emotional, dreamy sign that values fantasy and imagination. Create this spell jar to honor Pisces season and bring yourself out of the mundane, heavy humdrum of life by embracing the bright, imaginative magick of The Fish.

* Paper, green or blue preferred
* Writing tool, green or blue preferred
* The Moon tarot card (see notes)
* Clear quartz
* Moonstone
* Tektite
* Catnip
* Lilac
* Lily
* Full Moon Water (see page 160 for the Full Moon Water Spell Jar recipe)

1. On the paper, write an affirmation relating to the intrinsic qualities of Pisces that you're looking to magnify and embrace for yourself, such as, "I trust that my intuition guides me to where I'm meant to be. My creativity and heightened imagination attract empathetic, compassionate friendships."

2. Say the written affirmation aloud. Repeat until it truly resonates with you.

3. Add the written affirmations to the spell jar.

4. Add The Moon tarot card to the spell jar.

5. Add the clear quartz, moonstone, and tektite.

6. Add the catnip, lilac, and lily to the jar.

7. To activate the spell, fill the jar with enough Full Moon Water to submerge the ingredients.

Cosmic Spell Jars

8. Seal the spell jar using your preferred method.

To recharge this spell jar, place it in moonlight. Keep it on your bedside table or under your bed to promote message-bearing, intuitive dreams.

Notes: Know that this will be submerged in water, so a printed photo or drawn representation of The Moon tarot card will do if you don't want to sacrifice a professionally created tarot card for this spell jar.

Full Moon Water Spell Jar

The full moon phase is known as a very powerful, magickal time. The full moon is associated with manifestation, the realization of goals and dreams, and reaching your full potential. Honor and harness the power of the full moon with this spell jar.

The water from this spell jar can be used to enhance spells with the power of the full moon, but it is not intended to be consumed. If you'd like to make Full Moon Water to use in herbal teas and other magickal beverages, modify this spell by using only water that's safe to drink and placing the crystals and herbs around the jar to charge it instead of inside the water, to avoid any contamination.

✳ A full moon
✳ Water (see notes)
✳ Jasmine
✳ Willow
✳ Pumpkin seeds

✳ Evening primrose
✳ Crystals that heighten intuition and promote calm, loving, powerful energy, such as rose quartz, clear quartz, amethyst, and moonstone

1. On the evening of a full moon, ideally in the light of the full moon, pour the water into the spell jar.

2. Add the jasmine, willow, pumpkin seeds, and evening primrose to the jar.

3. Add the rose quartz, amethyst, and moonstone, or your crystals of choice, to the jar.

4. Seal the jar using your preferred method.

5. To activate this spell jar with the power of the full moon, place it outside on a windowsill, ideally directly in moonlight. Don't worry if the weather is cloudy, the spell jar will still soak in the magickal lunar vibes.

Incorporate the water from your Full Moon Water Spell Jar into other spellwork by using it to anoint candles or altars. You also can keep the jar sealed and meditate with it whenever you need an invigorating boost of full moon power. To recharge the jar, place it in the moonlight overnight.

Notes: I like to use natural water, such as melted snow, rainwater, or water from a stream or lake. Tap or purified water will work, too.

New Moon Water Spell Jar

Are you looking to switch to a new career? Begin a new relationship? Launch an entrepreneurial venture? The New Moon phase is the perfect time to begin journeys. The night of a New Moon holds potent magick that will help nurture any seeds you plant for the future. This spell jar is intended to be created during a New Moon, allowing you to harness the energy of that special night and make your plans come to fruition successfully.

- ✳ Paper, black and silver preferred
- ✳ Writing tool, black and silver preferred
- ✳ Crystals that offer support during periods of change and growth, such as garnet, kambaba jasper, and mookaite jasper
- ✳ Crystals specific to your goal for this spell (see notes)
- ✳ Acorn
- ✳ Chickweed
- ✳ Willow
- ✳ Water (see notes)
- ✳ Glitter in a color relating to the goal of your spell (see notes)

1. On the piece of paper, write an affirmation relating to your goal for this spell and the journey you're beginning. For example, if I were looking to find a new relationship, I might write, "I attract the right people into my life. My heart and mind are open to new connections and healthy, supportive relationships."

2. Speak the affirmation aloud. Repeat until you really feel that the words resonate with you.

3. Add the written affirmation to the spell jar.

4. Add the garnet, kambaba jasper, and mookaite jasper to the spell jar.

5. Add the crystals that resonate with your specific goal.

6. Add the acorn, chickweed, and willow.

7. To activate the spell, add enough water to the jar to submerge the ingredients. You can fill it completely, if you'd like.

8. Sprinkle glitter on top to symbolize luck and success.

9. Seal the spell jar using your preferred method.

Periodically give the spell jar a swirl to shake up any stagnant energy and reinvigorate its magickal energy and intentions.

Notes:

CRYSTALS: Use goal-specific crystals. For instance, if the journey you're looking to begin deals with love, choose crystals associated with love, such as morganite and/or rose quartz. If your goal involves attracting luck and wealth, use green jade and/or pyrite. See the Crystal Index on page 71 for more inspiration.

WATER: I like to use natural water, such as melted snow, rainwater, or water from a stream or lake. Tap or purified water will work, too.

GLITTER: See page 49 for the Color Correspondences chart to help you decide which color to use. White and iridescent are appropriate, all-purpose colors to use in this spell jar if you're having trouble deciding.

 Cosmic Spell Jars

Bibliography

Becker, M. J. (2005). "An Update on Colonial Witch Bottles." Digital Commons @ West Chester University. Retrieved August of 2022 from https://digitalcommons.wcupa.edu/anthrosoc_facpub/132/.

Becker, M. J. (2009). "An American Witch Bottle: Evidence for the Practice of 'White Witchcraft' in Colonial Pennsylvania." *Archaeology* magazine archive. Retrieved August of 2022 from https://archive.archaeology.org/online/features/halloween/witch_bottle.html.

Illes, Judika. *The Element Encyclopedia of 5000 Spells: The Ultimate Reference Book for the Magical Arts.* New York: Harper One, 2008.

Acknowledgments

This book was written while my four rescue dogs cuddled on plush beds under my desk, chewing on frozen Kong toys stuffed with pumpkin purée and blueberries. So, Kong, thank you for making the toys that kept my dogs occupied long enough for me to write this book!

To editors extraordinaire Casie Vogel and Kierra Sondereker of Ulysses Press, thank you for your expert, meticulous guidance. Kierra, your skilled eye and unparalleled editorial knowledge have proven invaluable to the creation of this book. I'm also very grateful to everyone else at Ulysses Press who worked diligently on its layout and perfected its mystical design.

I also want to express my appreciation and respect for author Judika Illes, whose immense tomes have offered immeasurable knowledge on the subject of witchcraft for decades. I first discovered her work when I was a preteen twenty years ago, when I'd sneak away from my strict Evangelical home to peruse the Alternative Spirituality section of a local bookshop in search of a path that resonated with me more fully. Thank you for the wisdom you've cultivated and shared with the world.

Without the dedication and innovation of my medical team, I wouldn't be here, continuing to achieve my lifelong dreams of authorship. Thank you particularly to Mayo Clinic internist Dr. Nadir Bhuiyan for his compassion and the thorough investigations he orchestrated, and to my brilliant neurophysiologist, Dr. Bake, and dedicated hematologist, Dr. Perez-Botero. I'd also like to extend my appreciation to the good folks at Cloud Nine Ergonomics for creating the adaptive keyboard that makes typing comfortable for me.

Acknowledgments need to be made to the many generations of spellcasters that came before us and paved our way, particularly to those who dared to create spell bottles under threat of persecution, because they truly understood their power and found spellcrafting to be worth the risk. Thank you for illuminating the path that led to modern witchcraft.

About the Author

Minerva Siegel is a writer, author, sensitivity reader, and longtime practitioner of witchcraft who haunts her Victorian home in Milwaukee, Wisconsin, with her gruff Taurean husband and their motley pack of rescue dogs. In addition to this book, she's the author of *Tarot for Self-Care: How to Use Tarot to Manifest Your Best Self, Houseplant Tarot, The Nightmare before Christmas Tarot Deck and Guidebook, The Labyrinth Tarot Deck and Guidebook, the Disney Villains Tarot Deck and Guidebook*, along with several other licensed tarot decks and their guidebooks published by Insight Editions.

Born in Seattle under a Sagittarian Sun and Capricorn Moon, Minerva enjoys crystal meditation, listening to low-fi indie and punk on an old record player in perpetual need of a new needle, and cultivating a magickal home. Minerva is also a disabled wheelchair user. Though the physical body has limitations, there's freedom and power in fully tapping into our own magickal potential. Her many guidebooks help readers do just that. You can find her on Instagram @Author.Minerva.Siegel.